AF413236

MARRIAGE
WAS NOT MY
BURDEN

Mbuyi Mukendi

Table of Contents

Chapter One:
The Weight of Gold

The gold bangle slid onto MuaBana's wrist not merely like a shackle, but with a sickening weight and a dull, resonant clink. A piercing sound that seemed to silence the already hushed living room. The bangle was a stunning piece of craftsmanship, with its thick coil of meticulously hammered gold. Its surface was filigreed with the geometric patterns of the Luba tradition, each curve and indent a testament to wealth and permanence.

It was a wedding gift from her future mother-in-law, a woman whose name was Madame Zola. A name spoken with the reverence reserved for minor royalty of the city, a name that opened doors and closed arguments before they could begin.

Madame Zola's smile was wide, almost too wide, and held long enough to feel deliberate. It curved sharply at the edges, a sliver of teeth peeking through, polished and precise, like a blade briefly unsheathed. Her dark eyes, heavy-lidded, were piercing in their stillness, the kind that measured rather than welcomed, that catalogued flaws and advantages with equal efficiency. There was no softness in her gaze, no warmth, only appraisal. The smile promised approval, but the eyes delivered possession, an airtight seal snapping shut around MuaBana's future.

The moment the gold kissed her skin, MuaBana felt a chilling contrast between its exterior warmth and the sudden coldness in her own chest. She tried to return the expected smile, but the muscles in her face felt stiff, unfamiliar with the easy, grateful expression of a demure bride. She wasn't cold; she was full of a hidden, furious heat—a furnace of unspoken rebellion that smoldered beneath the flawless silk of her tunic, threatening to burst the seams of polite society. The gold was beautiful, yes, but it didn't feel like an adornment. It felt deliberate. Measured. It felt like a leash, custom-made and exquisitely heavy.

"A woman's beauty is a gift to be guarded," her mother, Maman Bibishbo, had said just moments before, her voice a low, firm melody as she adjusted the flawless, cerulean drape of MuaBana's finest silk tunic. "But her true worth, MuaBana, is found in a good husband, a strong family, and the secure walls of a prosperous home."

Maman Bibishbo's hands, powerful and knowing, bearing the unseen evidence of decades spent grading papers and enveloping not just for her own dozen children but also for countless students and others in need of care, rested on MuaBana's shoulders. There was love in the touch, but also ownership, the firm assurance of a woman who believed survival itself depended on obedience. She gave MuaBana's shoulder a final, proprietary squeeze as she left MuaBana sitting in her room.

*****

Maman Bibishbo, a woman who had taught school for ten years before dedicating herself entirely to raising her formidable twelve children, knew the true, grinding weight of those words. She hadn't just taught lessons; she had lived them. MuaBana and her twin brother, KankoloNkonko, were the youngest. Their family of twelve—seven girls and five boys—was a chaotic, beautiful symphony in their sprawling home in Kananga, Zaïre. Their father, MukandaMoyo, a well-provided administrator for the national railroad, had ensured their lives were rich, not just with financial security, but with rigorous education and relentless activity, a household where ambition was encouraged as fiercely as competition, and idleness was treated almost like a moral failing.

The six-bedroom house, whose long hall led past the rain-used kitchen and the adjacent ironing-office to the majestic living room, served primarily for sleeping, receiving guests, and watching television. The house was generally quiet; its walls were not saturated with everyday scents, as the laundry room was detached and most cooking took place outside. Members spent their time in the open air, enjoying the sunshine and the breeze. This vibrant outdoor life occurred on the grounds, which were surrounded by abundant mango, avocado, and citrus trees.

2

Beyond the kitchen was a laundry room, and a small oratory dedicated to the family's faith—a quiet space of prayer, reverence, and tradition. Every evening at 8 PM, the family would gather there to pray, their voices rising in hymns of Tshiluba, French, and Latin.

In a dedicated area, Maman Bibishbo grew cassava, corn, yams, and herbs. Their backyard, a generous patch of well-designed clay earth, topped with beautiful small stones and a nice lawn, surrounded by a high hedge of bougainvillea and more mango trees, was a place of perpetual motion and noise, constantly being transformed—into a classroom, a debating hall, a field for soccer and volleyball, and most often, a whirlwind of shouts, flying bodies, and other games.

The household was also home to a menagerie of pets: two energetic dogs named Caesar and Michou, a sleek cat named Matou, and a number of chickens that roamed freely in the yard. Their maids lived in separate rooms, which included three spacious studios, a shared kitchen, and a bathroom. It was a place where tradition and modernity, order and chaos, coexisted in a delicate balance.

MuaBana and KankoloNkonko, who were both strikingly tall and leanly athletic, thrived in this beautiful maelstrom. But while KankoloNkonko preferred basketball, MuaBana had claimed soccer as her visceral truth. She did not choose it so much as recognize herself in it. It was on the sun-baked, uneven field that she was truly herself, where her mind finally quieted by the rhythmic pound of her own feet and the singular focus on the game. She cherished these moments, where life and noise dissolved into instinct and skill.

Just yesterday, she had been a blur of joyful defiance. She had slipped past her sturdy older brother, Mpetu, with a quick, deceptive feint and a burst of impossible speed. The ball was a shadow at her feet, speaking only to her, following her command. Her twin, KankoloNkonko, yelled a warning that MuaBana ignored, already anticipating the movement. Her eyes were solely on the ball. She took her shot, not with brute, masculine force, but with the elegant precision of someone who knew the exact angle, the precise power, and the spin required to defeat the physics of the moment. It was less an act of strength than of knowing.

It was as if time had come to a standstill. The moment the ball hit the makeshift net, a glorious smile spread across MuaBana's face. The clean, stunning victory. She took a breath; a rush of cool air filled her lungs. The satisfying thwack of the ball against the rusty, makeshift net was not just a win. It was a feeling of unadulterated, unassailable freedom, so brief it almost hurt. At that moment, she felt as if she were the master of her own destiny.

But the family's deep love of sport came with unspoken, deeply ingrained rules. For a girl, the sheer force and sweat of soccer was deemed too rough, too visible, too unladylike. Her parents, who held MuaBana's academic brilliance (she was consistently "first of the class," her report cards laminated with pride) so dear, had presented their arguments countless times: the risk of injury that could mar her "marriageable" looks, the potential for social scorn in a conservative community, and the time taken away from her proper studies. These were delivered gently, reasonably, as though concern itself were proof of correctness.

MuaBana knew that they didn't understand the complex mathematics of her soul. What made her ache? What made her ignite? What did she want and desire? It was as if all was for naught. They didn't understand that the game was a non-negotiable outlet for her pent-up energy, her gnawing frustration, and her intense, physical joy. Without it, her grades would inevitably plummet. For her, this was a silent, powerful, and utterly logical protest that always, eventually, won back her stolen ball.

Yet even the fierce, public passion of soccer was not the deepest part of her rebellion. There was something more. Something that MuaBana had kept close to her heart. Her true sanctuary, her private chapel, which lay hidden behind the kitchen's small, dilapidated utility room. It was a secret studio, a delicious, liberating mess of half-finished canvases, pots of fragrant, vibrant ochre and indigo mixed with water, and brushes stained with every shade imaginable.

It was hers, known only to her, and well, to some runaway mice, here and there. In her little sanctuary, the world's expectations could not reach her. She was not a daughter, a sister, or a prospective wife; she was simply an artist, a creator.

The only burden she ever felt in this room was the urgent, exhilarating need to capture the transient beauty of the world before it vanished. She had a half-finished portrait of the old Banyan tree from the central market. The portrait depicted its massive, aerial roots twisting into the dry earth like the arthritic knuckles of an ancient ancestor. It's rough, monumental energy mirrored her own internal struggle. She had painted it in stolen hours, sometimes racing against the daylight, sometimes in quiet moments of the early morning. Sometimes she would be afraid that if she stopped too long, the feeling would escape her.

She hadn't been able to work on it since the proposal arrived three weeks ago, the vibrant colors in the pots suddenly looking dull and meaningless. Her hands, which only yesterday could command a soccer ball with perfect grace, now felt too numb, too heavy—too weighted by the gold on her wrist and the expectations of her name.

The man, Mr. Kanga, was the embodiment of stability. He was well-regarded and enviably wealthy. His family owned the largest spice trade in the region, their warehouses filled with the intoxicating aromas of vanilla, cinnamon, and ginger, promising MuaBana a life of absolute security and respect. It was the kind of life that people envied without questioning.

Her parents often spoke of the expansive, cool house she would inhabit, the servants she would manage, and the respected life she would lead, as if describing a perfect, finished picture ripped from a magazine.

But when MuaBana closed her eyes, she didn't see a life of comfort. She saw only a blank canvas encased in a heavy, ornamental frame. Beautiful, yes, but already decided and not hers. It was not of her choice.

It was a life waiting to be filled in by someone else's hand and painted over with their colors, not her own vibrant palette. She looked down at her wrist, at the heavy, ornate gold bangle. The metal was still cool against her pounding pulse, a promise of a future she didn't want and a future she hadn't chosen. It felt like a noose was tightening around her neck.

The gold didn't feel like wealth, MuaBana thought again; it felt like a foreclosure on her identity. And MuaBana knew, with a certainty that was both terrifying and liberating, that marriage was not her burden. The true, suffocating burden was the expectation that she would simply accept it without a single word of protest, that she would cease to exist so that the wife could be born.

Chapter Two:
A New Horizon

The MukandaMoyo and Bibishbo home in Kananga was a sprawling, bustling hub of life. With six large bedrooms, a vast living and dining room that could comfortably seat the entire family and their many guests, and a long hallway that echoed with the sounds of their daily lives, the house felt less like a building and more like a universe unto itself. A small office sat conveniently next to the large kitchen, where their mother often planned lessons or balanced the household's books.

Beyond the kitchen was a laundry room, and a small oratory dedicated to the family's faith—a quiet space of prayer, reverence, and tradition. Every evening at 8 PM, the family gathered there to pray, their voices rising in hymns of Tshiluba, French, and Latin. The melodies shifted with the liturgical year, following the sacred rhythms of Ordinary Time, Advent, Christmas, Lent, and Easter.

The household was also home to a menagerie of pets: two energetic dogs named Caesar and Michou, a sleek cat named Matou, and a number of chickens that roamed freely in the yard. Their maids lived in separate rooms, which included three spacious studios, a shared kitchen, and a bathroom. It was a place where tradition and modernity, order and chaos, coexisted in a delicate balance.

Dinner that evening was a boisterous affair, as it always was in a house filled with fourteen people. The clatter of plates, the lively debates between siblings, and the steady hum of their father's conversation with their mother provided the familiar soundtrack to MuaBana's life. Yet, as she ate her fufu and savory stew, she felt a subtle tension simmering beneath the surface, a direct result of her victory on the field. Her mother's quiet glances and her father's more pointed questions about her schoolwork felt like a soft interrogation, a way of reminding her where her true priorities were meant to lie.

Later, as the house began to quiet down, MuaBana found herself in the cool, dimly lit hallway, leaning against the wall and staring out a window at the star-studded Kananga sky. She was lost in thought when she heard a low whistle from behind her.

It was Kongolo, her oldest brother and her confidant. He was already a doctor, a fact her parents never tired of mentioning, but he had a quiet rebelliousness that she admired. He saw her passion for soccer not as a distraction, but as a discipline.

"You have a way of making a spectacle out of a simple game, Mua," he said, a smile in his voice. "Another perfect shot."

"It wasn't a spectacle," she countered, a faint blush on her cheeks. "Just a good play."

"A play that has Maman and Papa worried about your future again," he said gently, moving to stand beside her. "They think you'll forget all of their plans for you. That your dream of playing will make you forget your books."

"They don't get it," MuaBana said, her voice dropping to a whisper. "My grades dropped because they wouldn't let me play. It's the other way around. The game helps me. It clears my head, Kongolo. When I'm on the field, I can think. Really think. It makes my mind sharper, it gives me a place to be free so I can focus on my studies."

Kongolo nodded, his expression serious. "I know. It's a concept they can't grasp. Their world was built on a different set of rules. For them, a good education for a girl means a good future and a respectable husband. They're still thinking about a traditional marriage for you, about a life where you're taken care of."

"I don't want to be 'taken care of.' I want to take care of myself," MuaBana said, the words coming out with a quiet force. "I want to be a doctor, like you, but I also want to play. I want both."

Kongolo looked at her, and his smile returned, this time with a hint of something new in the curve of his smile, almost secretive. She looked at her brother inquisitively. So, he told her.

Unbeknownst to her, the family had received a call earlier that day. MuaBana had been noticed. A recruiter for the national team had seen her play in a local exhibition match and wanted to bring her to Kinshasa to join a professional club for a final selection process. She was only sixteen, but she was a senior in high school, already studying business administration, and her talent was undeniable.

Listening to this, it was as if her heart was pounding in her chest. It felt like every nerve in her body had been lit on fire at once. MuaBana couldn't believe her ears. Her chest felt light, as if the news had lifted her entire being off the ground and into the sky. A rush of warmth spread from her heart to her fingers as she imagined.

The opportunity was extraordinary, but the family was at a standstill.

The news had thrown the house into a quiet chaos. The siblings were all ecstatic. They saw it as the fulfillment of her secret passion, a recognition of her relentless dedication. Her brothers were particularly supportive, having witnessed firsthand her natural talent and her struggle. Her older sister whispered in awe, imagining the city lights of Kinshasa and the fame that might follow, while her brothers practically argued amongst themselves about how best to support her. But their father was opposed. He saw a professional soccer career as a fleeting, unreliable path, something beneath the dignity of a woman of her academic caliber. A life in business, with a stable career and a good family, was the future he had always envisioned for her. The thought of his daughter traveling alone to the bustling, intimidating capital city was simply too much.

MuaBana stood in the hallway, the weight of the family's divided opinions pressing down on her. The conflict was no longer a personal battle between her and her parents, but a family-wide debate. On one side stood her father, a man who loved her fiercely but couldn't see beyond his own deeply held fears and expectations. On the other stood the rest of her family, a chorus of encouragement, pushing her towards a future that was bold and unknown.

It was a terrifying, exhilarating possibility. The risk was enormous, the potential for failure immense. Despite her father's disapproval, MuaBana made her choice. She would go to Kinshasa.

The morning she left, the air in the house was thick with unspoken tension. Everyone gathered in the living room for a final prayer before she departed, but her father was nowhere to be found. MuaBana stood with her suitcase, her siblings offering hugs and words of encouragement, but her eyes kept searching for him. She knew he was in his study, and a part of her hoped he would come out to say goodbye. A lump rose in her throat each time she thought she might see him in the doorway, a silent acknowledgment of the gap between her dreams and his fears. But he didn't.

She walked out the front door and down the driveway with her heavy bag, her heart aching with the silence. And yet, with every step, a strange lightness grew inside her. The pain of his refusal was real, a burden she would carry, but it was overshadowed by a fierce, determined joy. She was on her way to Kinshasa, and her future was finally, truly her own.

When her plane landed at N'djili Airport in Kinshasa, a delegation from the team was waiting for her. She had carried only a small bag over her shoulder, her strong legs on full display beneath a khaki skirt that fell just above her knees. She wore a simple yet beautiful tan short-sleeved T-shirt and sandals made of a denim-like cloth. Her hair was short on both sides, with more length on top, giving her a punkish, confident look that was breathtaking. Even as a stranger in a new city, she held herself with the posture of someone who knew her worth, who had fought for this very moment.

MuaBana was an innocent girl walking into an unknown world, and yet she was full of life and confidence. She greeted the people who had come to take her from the airport, and they took her to her mother's older sister, her Aunt Mere Djo, who lived not too far from the airport in the municipality of Kingasani-Mikondo. That is where she would spend her first night, the first of many to come, a world away from the familiar comfort of her family home.

It was July, and MuaBana was acutely aware of the difference in climate between the two cities. In Kananga, the dry season made the air crisp and pleasant, with night temperatures that could drop as low as 45°F. But Kinshasa was hot and heavy, the air thick with humidity even during its short dry season, and the nights only cooled to a balmy 65°F. Her skin stuck to her clothes in a way that made her cringe at first, but she reminded herself that this was the cost of stepping into the bigger world.

The constant damp heat was a physical reminder that she was no longer in the familiar landscape of her childhood. She was hot all the time, a constant layer of sweat clinging to her skin. But she got used to it. The discomfort faded into the background as her new life took shape, a demanding rhythm that she embraced wholeheartedly.

Her days were a relentless and beautiful cycle. She would wake up at 5 AM for a morning workout with the team, pushing her body to its limits as the sun began to rise. Afterward, she would go to school, her mind sharp and focused, proving once again that her passion fueled her academic success, not hindered it. After her classes, she would return to the field for another practice around 4 PM, not getting home until a bit after 8 PM, where she would study and prepare to do it all over again the next day.

Some nights, she collapsed onto the small, unfamiliar bed, exhausted to the bone, but the glow of possibility kept her awake long enough to make plans for the next day.

MuaBana was happy. She was exhausted, but she was fulfilled, living out the dream she had fought so hard for. There was only one thing that disturbed her peace: her father's silence. She wrote to him often, long, detailed letters about her life, her studies, and her teammates, but he never responded. The weight of his disapproval was the only burden she had carried with her on this journey, a lingering sadness in an otherwise joyful new life.

She continued this demanding routine throughout the summer, preparing for the upcoming season with the determination that had earned her the nickname "She who knows it all."

The rigorous training, combined with her dedication to her studies, paid off. When the time came for her final exams, she was ready. She succeeded, obtaining her High School diploma with the same academic prowess she had always shown. Now, with her education secured and her skills honed, she was poised to compete in the qualifying games for the African Championship, ready to show her father and the world what she was capable of.

Chapter Three:
The Unspoken Burden

The rhythm of Kinshasa was a frantic, demanding beat, but MuaBana embraced it. It seemed to pulse beneath her feet, every honking car and shouting street vendor a drumbeat to her own relentless tempo. Her life was a relentless cycle of early-morning training, classes, and late-afternoon practice under the unforgiving sun. The air itself seemed to push against her skin, thick with humidity, carrying the smell of the river, exhaust, and sizzling street food, a constant reminder that she was far from the quiet streets of Kananga.

The heat of the city, once a physical shock, had become a constant companion, much like the ache in her muscles and the fierce satisfaction she felt after a well-played game. On the field, with the ball at her feet, she was free. The world of expectations and traditional duties melted away, replaced by the simple, beautiful logic of the game: skill, strategy, and pure, unbridled effort.

Her teammates, a vibrant group of young women from all walks of life, had quickly become her new family. Their laughter often rang louder than the city itself, a comforting noise that filled the empty spaces in her apartment and the ache in her chest on lonely evenings. They were a chorus of support, their cheers and shared laughter a welcome balm to the homesickness that, at times, felt like a physical weight in her chest. Sometimes, after practice, they would linger on the sidelines, joking and comparing scrapes and bruises, their camaraderie stitching together a sense of belonging she hadn't realized she craved so deeply. They spoke her language, both on and off the field, a language of ambition and fierce independence.

But there was a silent burden she carried, heavier than any bag she had packed. The letters she wrote to her father, filled with detailed accounts of her victories, her newfound friends, and her academic progress, were met with an unyielding silence. Each letter folded and sealed, a careful construction of words meant to bridge a gap that felt impossible to cross, seemed to vanish into an invisible wall. She imagined him reading them, frowning in disapproval, shaking his head silently at the daughter who dared to choose her own path.

Her mother and siblings sent replies, their words a mix of affection and shared news from home, but her father's absence was a deafening void. Each time she wrote, she poured her heart onto the page, hoping her words would be enough to bridge the distance, to prove to him that her path was not a fleeting passion but a serious, life-affirming pursuit. She could feel her pulse quicken as she sealed the envelopes, a mixture of hope and fear fluttering in her stomach, wondering if this time, finally, he might hear her.

She would train harder, run faster, and study longer, driven by a desperate need to make him proud. Each goal she scored was a small, silent scream into the void, a plea for his understanding. After practice, when the stadium emptied and the city lights flickered on across the horizon, she would linger alone, feeling the ache in her legs and the rhythm of her heart as if it were a heartbeat sent straight to him. Her discipline was a quiet protest, a way of saying, "This is who I am. This is what I was meant to do."

She was determined to prove that a woman could build her own life, on her own terms, and that her dreams were not a rejection of his love, but a reflection of the strength he had always told her she possessed.

She was happy in her new life, but the joy was always shadowed by the unrequited hope that one day, he would answer. Some nights, she would lie awake, listening to the distant horns and shouting vendors outside, and imagine his voice reading her words. Her chest ached with longing, a mix of love and stubborn pride that made sleep difficult. It was a burden she had chosen, but that didn't make it any less heavy. She was a professional athlete in training, a brilliant student, and a determined young woman, but she was still, at her core, a daughter who longed for her father's approval.

The unrequited hope MuaBana carried was finally laid to rest a few weeks later. In a stunning, hard-fought match, she and her team won the African Women's Soccer Championship, bringing the trophy home to the Democratic Republic of Congo. When the final whistle blew, she sank to her knees on the field, sweat stinging her eyes, and felt tears blur her vision. The weight of months of struggle, of letters sent into silence, of every lonely evening training alone, seemed to lift for the first time.

A few weeks later, MuaBana returned to her maternal home, both happy with her victory and yet uncertain of what to expect from her father. She sat by her mother in the sprawling backyard of their big house in Kananga, her nerves a tight knot in her stomach. The scent of fresh cassava and ripening mangoes hung in the warm afternoon air, a quiet reminder of the life she had left behind, and a comfort she clung to in her anxiety.

Around 4:45 PM, the usual time, her dad, who had stopped driving and preferred walking to work, walked in. A chorus of "Bonsoir Papa" greeted him, and he answered each of his children, blessing them on their foreheads.

MuaBana was the last. When her father saw her, he was very surprised and embraced her tightly. The embrace was strong, but for the first time it carried not disapproval, not warning, but pride and relief, and she felt the years of silence dissolve in that single, firm hold. The family gathered around, a symphony of wiping tears, hugging, and laughing as they celebrated. Finally, MuaBana was relieved.

The next day, her father invited her to his office. Sunlight streamed through the tall office windows, glinting off the polished wood of his desk, and for a moment, the room felt smaller, warmer, less formal than she had imagined. Her father was the director of the human resources bureau for the railroad company. All his colleagues came to the office, and he presented his daughter with a broad smile. They all celebrated MuaBana, having watched her triumph on television. It was in that moment that MuaBana discovered her father had been following her progress from afar, yet had been too hurt by her choice to respond to her letters.

MuaBana remained with her family for a whole month, a time of healing and shared joy. She walked the familiar paths of the backyard, her bare feet sinking into the soft earth, feeling the comfort of home, laughter, and conversation mingling like sunlight through the trees. Each evening, she sat under the old mango tree, sipping warm tea with her mother, savoring the simple, tangible love that had always surrounded her. She returned to Kinshasa, this time, relieved and happier, her burdens lifted, and her path made clear.

Chapter Four:
The Fateful Telegram

MuaBana returned to Kinshasa in a state of grace. The heavy silence between her and her father had been shattered, replaced by a shared, if still delicate, pride. She trained with a renewed intensity, the field no longer a battlefield for her father's approval, but simply a place of pure, joyful competition. Each sprint, each pass, each goal was a celebration, a quiet acknowledgment of her own hard-won freedom. The air carried the tang of sweat and dust, the shouts of teammates, and the distant rumble of the city—sounds that now felt like a symphony rather than a pressure.

She spent the next year building her career, her name growing in prominence across the continent. She was nineteen now, her talent undeniable, her life wholly her own. When she flew home to Kananga for the annual December holiday, she arrived not as the runaway student but as the decorated champion. The familiar streets seemed smaller somehow, quieter, yet her heart felt lighter, a thrill of belonging and triumph vibrating in her chest. She noticed the smell of roasted corn on the sidewalks, the sun cutting through the courtyard just right, and she smiled at how much she had missed the gentle chaos of home.

The family celebration was louder and more chaotic than ever, her victory the central topic of every conversation. Her father, proud and expansive, told the story of her championship match to every relative who stepped through the door. She watched him speak, the lines of his face softening as he recounted her clever moves on the field, and for a moment she felt the warmth of his pride wrap around her like a cloak. The only thing that had changed, it seemed, was that the family's gentle worries about her future had been replaced by a communal confidence.

She had found her path.

It was this sense of peace, this feeling of having finally earned her freedom, that made the arrival of the telegram, a formal marriage request delivered through the family network, all the more devastating.

*****

MuaBana was sitting in the backyard, sketching on a large sheet of paper, not the knots of frustration she used to draw, but bold, sweeping lines of movement and color inspired by her life on the field. Her fingers traced the curves of a figure mid-kick, the brush of charcoal over the page echoing the rhythm of her heartbeat. The wind teased at her hair, carrying the scent of cassava leaves and the distant hum of the market. The air was dry and cool, a welcome contrast to Kinshasa.

Her mother, Maman Bibishbo, emerged from the house holding a stiff, official-looking envelope. Her face was a study in restraint, her usual energy subdued, a quiet gravity in the way she moved that made MuaBana's chest tighten.

"MuaBana," she said, her voice softer than usual. "Please come inside. Your father and I need to speak with you."

The sketch forgotten, MuaBana followed her mother into the cool silence of the living room. Her father was seated on the heavy, carved sofa, his hands folded over a similar envelope. The room smelled faintly of polished wood and wax, a comforting scent that contrasted sharply with the tension that seemed to press down on her shoulders. The atmosphere was thick, solemn, like a church before a funeral. This was not the joyous pride of a week ago; this was the language of duty.

"Sit, my daughter," her father said, gesturing to the armchair opposite him.

MuaBana sat, the fine hair on her arms rising. "Papa, what is it?"

He placed the envelope on the low wooden table. "Mua, you are a woman of immense strength. You have proven that your mind is sharp and your will is powerful. We are proud of the woman you have become. You have achieved your academic goal, and you have achieved your athletic goal. Now, you must secure the final, and most important, part of your life."

Maman Bibishbo sat beside him, laying a hand on his arm. Her fingers were warm, but the gesture was heavy with expectation, a quiet reminder of the world MuaBana had been born into. "Your Auntie Mere Jo... she has been speaking with the family of Mister Etumba Ekonzo."

The name landed like a stone in the silent room. Etumba Ekonzo.

It was a name weighted with wealth, tradition, and a future mapped out without her consent. Her stomach sank, a cold ripple traveling through her body. He was a man in his mid-thirties, an established businessman in the city and heir to one of the region's oldest and wealthiest land-owning families. He was respected, successful, and politically connected. A "catch" by any community measure.

"They have formally requested your hand in marriage," her father continued, his voice regaining its administrative tone, placing the formal marriage proposal in front of her. "This is not a proposal of affection, Mua. This is a union of families, a path to security and respect that goes beyond any game or degree. It is an honor for our house."

MuaBana stared at the telegram, a stiff, official envelope containing the formal marriage proposal; her breath caught in her throat. Her hands trembled slightly, as though the paper itself was too heavy to hold. The sketches, the freedom, the years of struggle and self-definition, they all seemed distant as if all of it felt suddenly fragile, like sand slipping through her fingers. Her mind raced, rejecting the words, trying to connect them to the life she had just built.

"But... Papa. I don't know him. I have my career. I am going to university next year. I haven't even finished my business degree!"

"That is all still possible," her mother interjected quickly, handing the envelope to MuaBana. "Etumba Ekonzo's family is progressive. He will ensure you are comfortable, MuaBana. Your future will be set in stone. You will bring honor to our family name, secure your children's future, and live a life without want."

Her father leaned forward, his expression earnest. "Your talent, your education—these are wonderful ornaments, MuaBana. But they are a risk. This marriage is stability. It is your destiny. We have negotiated the terms, and the agreement is favorable. We have told them you will accept."

The weight of his words was heavier than any opposing player, heavier than the cold air of his initial disapproval.

We have told them you will accept.

The words rang in her mind, over and over again.

The soccer championship, the months of training, the hard-won freedom—it all seemed to vanish in the face of this single, absolute expectation. Her father had given her the space to pursue her passion, but he had never relinquished his right to define her purpose. It pressed on her chest, a suffocating mix of pride, fear, and disbelief. The freedom she had fought for seemed to blur, a distant memory caught in the corner of her vision.

MuaBana stood up, the chair scraping sharply on the tiled floor. Her eyes darted in the direction of the sketch she had left behind outside, the bold lines mocking her, a visual echo of the autonomy that now felt threatened.

"Marriage is not my burden to bear," she finally said, the words a strained whisper.

But as she looked at the sharp outline of the envelope, at the expectant faces of the two people she loved most, she knew the terrible truth: The marriage itself was not a burden; the burden was the obligation to live a life she had not chosen, to trade her pulse, her fire, her own uncharted path for a scripted future.

Her heart ached with the knowledge that freedom could be so close, yet still beyond reach.

*****

MuaBana spent the night in a state of suspended animation, tossing and turning on her bed as the shadows from the moonlight played across the walls, her thoughts spinning like the propellers she longed to command. Each time she closed her eyes, she saw herself strapped into a cockpit, soaring above the clouds, then the weight of the letter pulled her back down, crushing her chest. The news of the impending marriage proposal made the air in the house feel heavy and suffocating.

She finally understood the distinction she had whispered to herself in the garden: the marriage was not her burden; there was no obligation on her to give up her life for it.

The next morning, she sought out her father in his study.

Her mother was already there, her presence a silent, just standing with her hands folded, her expression carefully composed, a quiet armor of tradition that MuaBana felt closing in around her.

"Papa, Maman," MuaBana began, standing stiffly before the desk. Her fists were clenched at her sides, and a tremor ran through her voice, betraying the anger and fear she barely contained. "You need to withdraw your agreement for this proposal, Abba. I cannot marry Etumba Ekonzo."

Her father calmly set down the account ledger he was holding. The sound of the paper touching the polished desk seemed louder than it should, punctuating the stillness of the room. "MuaBana, we discussed this. The arrangement has been made. What is the issue?"

"The issue is my life," she said, her voice strained. Her chest heaved slightly, the words clawing their way out like sparks from a flame she could no longer contain. "You allowed me to go to Kinshasa because I proved I could pursue soccer and my studies. I secured my diploma and won a championship. I proved I can choose a life that makes me happy and succeed at it."

"And we are immensely proud of you," her father affirmed, with the finality of a judge. "But that was one chapter. This is the next. Your future is not a game you play; it is a foundation you lay. This marriage will provide the strongest foundation available."

"But my life isn't on the ground," MuaBana insisted, her voice trembling slightly with the weight of her conviction. Her gaze locked on her father's, searching for a flicker of understanding, any hint that he might see the fire burning inside her. "I have a career I want. I have spent the last year applying to flight schools. My true goal, what I have been preparing for since I was a child, is to become a pilot."

Her mother looked bewildered. "A pilot? What is she saying, Papa? A pilot? Like the men who fly the large commercial jets?"

MuaBana ignored her mother and addressed her father, trying to convey the enormity of her dream, her voice dropping to a sharper, urgent timbre, like the whine of an engine taking off. "I don't just want to fly; I want to command. I have the aptitude, the focus, and the discipline. I was studying Business Administration not just for a degree, but to understand the logistics of aviation. It is a career that demands excellence, and I am ready to give it."

Her father picked up the stiff, expensive envelope containing the Ekonzo proposal. He didn't look angry, only disappointed by her naivety.

"So," he summarized, his tone devoid of malice, but full of patronizing dismissal. "You want to refuse the hand of a respectable, successful man, whose family can guarantee your security for life, so that you can sit in a cockpit, amongst men, and be subjected to the risks and the schedule of a man's profession? You think a woman can manage a career in the air and still be a respectable wife and mother?"

"I will define what a respectable wife and mother is for myself!" MuaBana cried, her frustration bubbling over. "This is not a 'childish hobby,' Maman. It is a professional career, a necessary one! The world is changing. I want to be part of the change, not bound by the traditions of the past."

Maman Bibishbo reached out, her face a mask of worry. Her fingers grazed MuaBana's arm, a gesture of both care and caution, but it only made her recoil slightly. "MuaBana, the sky is for the birds and for the men who carry the great cargo. The ground is for a woman. Your place is here, secured. This marriage is stability. It is your destiny. You will bring honor to this house and to your husband's name. You can still study business; you can help your husband run his companies. But you will not trade reality for a dream that will only bring you trouble."

"My career is my reality! My future is in the air!" Her voice cracked, a high, raw note of desperation that echoed in the study like a bell tolling for a freedom denied.

"No," her father countered, placing a firm, final hand on the desk. "Your soccer was a passion we allowed you to indulge because you secured your education. This talk of flying is an unnecessary risk, a flirtation with a dangerous world that is not meant for you. The chapter on rebellion is closed, Mua. This is a matter of duty. You will marry the man who can provide the life you deserve, and you will stop pursuing a job that will only make you an outcast."

His words hit her with crushing certainty.

The room seemed to shrink around her, walls pressing in, the sunlight through the window harsh and accusing. Her dreams, once soaring, felt clipped and bound by invisible chains. They hadn't validated her freedom; they had merely granted a temporary reprieve.

Her dream of flying, which felt like the very center of her identity, was dismissed as a dangerous folly. Her throat burned, her eyes stung with unshed tears, but she swallowed them, feeling the bitter taste of resignation before it had even settled. The conversation was over before it had begun. The door to reason was sealed shut.

Chapter Five:
A Glimpse of the Sky

The air in the Bibishbo home felt dense, pressing in on MuaBana since the confrontation. Even the sunlight streaming through the windows seemed filtered, heavy with expectation, making the walls close in as she moved through the familiar rooms. Every loving glance from her mother, every firm but proud stare from her father, felt like a chain securing her to the destiny of Mrs. Etumba Ekonzo. Her chest ached, her lungs craving air that seemed just out of reach. She felt like a bird perched too long in a gilded cage, wings aching, ready to beat against confinement. She needed air, literal and metaphorical.

She found her escape not on the soccer pitch, the thought of playing felt shallow now, but in the familiar chaos of the local market, the same market where she had once ducked into alleys to avoid chores. The smells of drying fish, roasted peanuts, and dust-filled sunlight were almost intoxicating, grounding her in the rawness of life outside her parents' expectations. She wasn't avoiding chores today; she was seeking a way to avoid her life.

She paused near a stall selling carved wooden animals and masks. The colors of the carvings were vibrant against the muted dust of the market, and their silent, still forms felt alive in contrast to the static weight she carried in her chest.

The craftsman, a young man with hands as sturdy and precise as her brother Mpetu's, was meticulously sanding a small, stylized bird. He wore a simple, dust-covered work tunic, but his eyes were bright, constantly scanning the crowd with an easy curiosity. There was a rhythm to his movements, the quiet scratch of sandpaper on wood, that somehow spoke to the careful discipline MuaBana craved. This was DeMuke.

MuaBana, lost in her thoughts, almost knocked over a stack of his finished carvings.

"Careful," DeMuke said, his voice a low, friendly rumble. It was soft, almost teasing, but it carried an undertone of knowing. "Those birds already took flight in my mind. No need for them to take an unplanned flight here on the ground."

MuaBana mumbled an apology, immediately drawn to the carving in his hand. Her fingers twitched, craving the tactile proof of freedom she could feel in the smooth curves of the wood. "That one is beautiful. The wings are so delicate."

"Thank you. But they are trapped wings, aren't they?" DeMuke placed the wooden bird down. He looked at MuaBana, his head tilted slightly. "And you look like someone who knows exactly what trapped wings feel like. I see it in the way you look up. You're trying to calculate the wind speed."

MuaBana stiffened, unused to such observation. "I don't know what you mean."

DeMuke smiled, but it didn't reach his eyes; it was a smile of shared knowing. "I travel. I move things. I fix things. I tell stories about where I've been and what I've seen. And I've seen that look before. It's the look of someone whose most important life is happening somewhere else. For you, it's not far—it's high."

He was the first person since her soccer win who didn't mention her parents or the championship. He didn't measure her against anyone's expectations. He measured her against herself. He saw the core desire, the thing her family had just dismissed. She felt an urgent, reckless need to confess.

"I want to fly," she whispered, leaning closer, glancing quickly around the stall. Her voice trembled slightly, carrying the fear of being overheard but also the thrill of claiming her truth aloud. "I want to be a pilot."

DeMuke didn't blink. He reached beneath his crate and pulled out a worn, much-folded piece of paper.

"A pilot," he repeated, his tone respectful, entirely serious. "A noble calling. But the best training, the kind that will get you into the largest planes, is not here, is it?"

"No," MuaBana admitted, her throat tightening. "I need to go back to America. I need a real flight school. I've been looking at the Tuskegee Aerospace Science Program. My brother Kongolo knows people who said..." She trailed off, realizing she was sharing a secret plan with a stranger. Her voice trembled slightly, carrying the fear of being overheard but also the thrill of claiming her truth aloud.

DeMuke unfolded the paper. It wasn't a map or a manifest; it was a rough drawing of a sprawling campus complex.

"Tuskegee is a storied place," he said, tapping the drawing with his finger. "Not just for pilots, but for those who defied what the world said was possible. I spent a summer working construction nearby, near Alabama. I know the airport, and I know people who move between here and the States. People who don't ask questions about what a woman is *supposed* to be doing."

He pushed the paper across the counter toward her. "The problem, as I see it, is not about finding the school. The problem is getting there without your family's permission, which requires cash, a ticket, and a story that gets you past your father's watchful eye. A plane ticket to the States is a small fortune. Are you willing to trade everything here for the chance to climb into the cockpit?"

MuaBana looked from the diagram of the distant, hopeful campus to DeMuke's knowing face. Her chest felt tight with both longing and fear; the world she had dreamed of was within reach, yet so fragile. He wasn't encouraging a hobby; he was offering a practical route to a professional future. He was a piece of the outside world, a key to the cage she suddenly realized she was in.

"I am," she said, her voice clear and steady. She inhaled deeply, tasting the dust and sunlight, grounding herself, preparing for the leap. "I have my championship bonus saved. It's enough for a ticket and a month's rent. The only thing I can't find is the right path out."

"Then you haven't found the right storyteller yet," DeMuke said, collecting the diagram and handing her a small, smoothly sanded wooden bird. It felt cool and solid in her hand, a tangible token of hope, a tiny promise of the sky. "This is not a cage. This is a promise. Come back to the market tomorrow, after the sun is at its highest. We'll talk about logistics. We'll talk about how to get your feet off the ground."

Chapter Six:
The Official Flight Plan

MuaBana met DeMuke again beneath the great Tamarind tree. He had provided her with the name of a contact in Kinshasa—a cargo pilot who was sympathetic to her dream—and details about cheap, necessary travel documents. She had the cash, the ticket plan, and the logistical map. But the final, most crucial piece of the plan was still missing: the official acceptance from the Tuskegee Aerospace Science Program in Macon County, Alabama, United States. Without it, she was just running away to chase a wish. With it, she would build a career. Real flights needed dates, permissions, stamps, and signatures, DeMuke had said, tapping his finger against the wood. Dreams needed clearance, too.

The air in the house was thick with wedding preparations. Auntie MereJo had returned, bringing a host of well-meaning but suffocating relatives. They spoke in hushed, admiring tones of Etumba Ekonzo's properties and pedigree, and MuaBana's forthcoming role as the mistress of a powerful household. Every compliment felt like a rope being gently, politely tightened around her future. The pressure was a physical weight, but MuaBana met it with a strange, cool composure, like an athlete conserving energy before a final sprint.

Then, one Tuesday, it arrived.

A small, official envelope, addressed to her in the looping, formal script of the Tuskegee Institute Registrar's Office, sat on the mahogany console table in the hallway. Her mother had put it there, assuming it was a late correspondence regarding her past academic records.

MuaBana snatched it up the moment she was alone, retreating to the solitude of her old shared bedroom. Her twin brother, KankoloNkonko, was at school, and the house was momentarily quiet.

Her hands trembled as she tore open the envelope. Inside was a single, crisp letter bearing the college's seal. Her eyes scanned the text, stopping on the bolded, triumphant sentence:

"It is with immense pleasure that the Admissions Committee offers you a place in the upcoming cohort of the Tuskegee Aerospace Science Program, beginning in the Fall semester."

The air rushed out of her lungs in a silent whoosh of pure relief and fierce joy. It wasn't just an acceptance; it was validation. It was the confirmation that her dream was not a flight of fancy, but a qualified, achievable destiny. The date on the letter was only three weeks away—her window of escape was narrow, but defined. It had to be enough. She hoped it would be enough for DeMuke to arrange everything easily. Enough time for dreams to become real.

The letter was the official authorization for her life. She was no longer just defying her parents; she was choosing a *future*.

She walked out of the room, the letter clutched tightly, and found her father in the backyard, inspecting the vegetable garden with his foreman. MuaBana approached him, her spine straight, her expression resolved. Her heart beat the way it did before a decisive match—fast, controlled, unyielding.

"Papa," she said, her voice cutting through the quiet hum of the afternoon.

He looked up, surprised by her tone. "MuaBana? What is it?"

She held out the letter, not offering it, but displaying the seal. "I am not going to marry Etumba Ekonzo."

The words landed before the meaning could soften them. Her father dropped the pruning shears he was holding. Maman Bibishbo appeared on the porch, drawn by the sudden tension.

"We have gone over this," her father said, regaining his composure with a visible effort. His face twisted with concealed anger as he said, "The discussions are done. The date is being set."

"No," MuaBana countered. "I have made my choice. I am going to the United States. I have been accepted to the Tuskegee Aerospace Science Program."

She finally offered the letter. Her father took it, his face turning hard as he read the words of welcome.

"This is madness!" he bellowed, crumpling the paper slightly, but thankfully not tearing it, "You are nineteen years old! You will not travel across the world alone for this... this fantasy!"

"It is not a fantasy, Papa. It is the beginning of my career. And I will not go as a runaway. I am telling you my plan because I respect you and because you taught me to be strong enough to make my own decisions."

Her voice did not shake. That frightened him more than shouting ever could. She looked straight into his eyes, not pleading, but stating a fact. "I have enough of my soccer money to cover my flight and my first month's housing. I will enroll, I will work, and I will become a pilot. I will not bring shame to your name, and I will not disappear from this family. I promise you, I will return when my program is complete—a pilot, and a woman who built her own life."

Maman Bibishbo gasped, covering her mouth with her hand. Her father stared at the letter, then at MuaBana, the lines of pride and betrayal warring across his face. He saw the strength he had fostered in her, now wielded against him.

"If you walk out that door for this," her father finally said, his voice low and dangerous, "you do not come back until you are ready to live the life we chose for you."

MuaBana took a deep breath, the smell of fresh earth and ripe fruit in the air. "I will come back when I have earned my wings, Papa. And that is the only life I will ever live."

Chapter Seven:
The Cost of the Sky

The dinner that evening was not a celebration; it was an inquest. The long mahogany table, usually a stage for raucous debates and easy laughter, was a battleground. News of MuaBana's declaration had spread through the family like wildfire, fueled by Maman Bibishbo's tearful distress and Papa's thunderous silence.

No one asked her if she was hungry. Plates were filled anyway. The scrape of cutlery sounded louder than usual, metal against ceramic, impatient, judgmental. MuaBana sat, the Tuskegee acceptance letter now safely tucked away in her jacket pocket, feeling the collective gaze of her fifteen relatives. Papa presided at the head of the table, an unreadable mask of cold displeasure. Auntie MereJo, seated to MuaBana's left, started the assault.

"It is a slap in the face to your family, MuaBana," Auntie MereJo said, her voice dripping with disappointed virtue. "To a man who offered to give you the world. Do you know the honor Etumba Ekonzo's name would bring us? A pilot! It is reckless, *unseemly* work for a married woman."

MuaBana looked directly at her aunt. "I will not be a married woman. I will be a pilot. And I am capable of earning my own honor." A murmur of agreement moved down the table, quiet but sharp.

"But who will employ a woman?" asked an older cousin, shaking his head. "They will give the jobs to men. You will go to America, spend all your money, and return here with nothing but shame, too old and too willful for a good husband."

The silence that followed was broken by an unexpected voice: KankoloNkonko, her twin brother. "She will not fail. We've seen her work. When she sets her mind on the goal, she takes it. If Papa was allowed to leave for school, why can't Mua go for her career?"

MuaBana didn't look at him, but she felt the weight shift slightly in her chest.

"This is different, KankoloNkonko," Papa said, his voice low and dangerous. "My education secured your place here. Her flight... it *removes* her. It is a rebellion against the natural order of her life."

He did not look at MuaBana when he said it. But KankoloNkonko's defense had broken the dam. One by one, her siblings rallied. Kongolo, her oldest brother, spoke with the cool logic of a doctor. "Papa, the world is changing. The demand for qualified commercial pilots is global. MuaBana is brilliant. To force her into a domestic role that will smother her talent is the true waste. You taught us to pursue excellence, not comfort."

The final, and most shocking, support came from her mother. Maman Bibishbo set down her cutlery with a sharp *clink*. The sound cut through the room like a signal. Her eyes were red, but her posture was resolute.

"I have wept for two days," Maman Bibishbo admitted, her voice trembling but steady. "Because I fear for her safety and her loneliness. But my children's happiness is the only true honor I require. I will not see her spirit die in my house. MuaBana has the strength to accomplish this. You must accept that she will use it. She is going to Tuskegee. We will support her in our hearts, even if we cannot in our words."

Auntie MereJo gasped. Papa, stunned by his wife's public defiance, said nothing more.

No one spoke to her after that. The silence followed her out of the room.

The lines of division were clear: the siblings and the mother, united by love for her future; the father and the tradition-bound relatives, bound by fear of change.

MuaBana knew she had won the emotional battle, but the physical escape was still a treacherous path.

*****

The next day, with afternoon sun in the sky, MuaBana told her family she was taking a walk to clear her head. She had her bag packed and hidden near the back gate, and a taxi waiting discreetly down the road. Her final destination was the busy corner near DeMuke's market stall.

Every step away from the house felt deliberate, counted. When she arrived, DeMuke was not carving wood. He was waiting with a small, discreet man wearing a jacket with the logo of a local travel agency. That alone told her how serious this had become.

"MuaBana," DeMuke said, his eyes conveying respect for her audacity. "This is Mister Lenga. He has secured the ticket for the flight departing for Atlanta tomorrow evening."

Mister Lenga handed her a thick, unmarked envelope. "One ticket, registered under a slightly different spelling of your middle name, just in case. The passport and visa are valid. Your father has influence, but he will not be able to stop a flight that is already booked and confirmed."

MuaBana handed over the championship bonus money—a daunting stack of bills that represented years of sacrifice and the only security she possessed. Her hands lingered on the last note for a fraction of a second before letting go.

The cost of freedom, she thought, as the money left her hand.

"There is one more thing," DeMuke said. He reached into his pocket and pulled out a battered, laminated photo. It was a picture of a magnificent commercial jet, soaring over a lush, green landscape. The photo was creased at the corners, carried often, and handled with care. In the foreground, a woman in a pilot's uniform stood smiling.

"That is my sister," DeMuke explained. "She flies cargo for a large company out of Addis Ababa. When I told her about you, she wanted you to have this." He flipped the photo over. Scrawled on the back was a phone number and a single word: *"Go."*

MuaBana felt a rush of emotion, a powerful mix of terror and gratitude. She was truly not alone.

"You must go now," DeMuke urged, glancing nervously toward the main road. "Your father's influence starts here. The sooner you reach the capital, the safer you are."

As if on cue, a large, dark sedan—the kind Papa's company used— rounded the corner too fast. MuaBana's heart slammed against her ribs. For a split second, she froze.

"Go!" DeMuke shouted, practically shoving her into the shadows of the alley. "Run! Godspeed, future pilot!"

MuaBana didn't look back. Clutching the envelope and the precious photo, she sprinted through the maze of the market, the noise and smells blurring around her. Someone shouted. A cart rattled. A hand brushed her arm.

She ran until she reached the corner where the pre-arranged taxi was waiting. She threw open the door, dove inside, and shouted her destination: "The airport!"

The driver did not ask questions. He just drove. As the taxi pulled away, gaining speed on the dusty road toward the distant Kinshasa airport, MuaBana looked at the ticket in her hand. It was the physical embodiment of the promise she had made to herself and her mother: to return with her wings, unbound by the past.

The burden was cast off. The sky was calling.

Chapter Eight:
The Weight of Freedom

The landing was seamless, a soft kiss of the wheels against the Atlanta tarmac. MuaBana felt the subtle pressure change in the cabin—a sensation that, for the first time, felt like potential instead of peril. She wasn't just a passenger; she was a future colleague.

She stayed seated a moment longer than necessary, listening to the engines wind down, memorizing the sound. But the moment she stepped off the plane, the intoxicating scent of jet fuel and ambition was replaced by the crushing weight of reality. Atlanta's Hartsfield-Jackson was a sprawling, dizzying labyrinth compared to Kinshasa's N'djili. The sheer scale and speed of everything—the flashing signs, the hurried, impersonal faces, the chilling roar of the air conditioning—made her feel small and very, very foreign. People moved around her without meeting her eyes. No one noticed she was afraid.

She took a bus south, a lonely, hours-long journey to the quieter, historic town of Tuskegee, Alabama. The transition from the dry, clear air of Kananga to the heavy, humid heat of the American South was jarring. The heat was familiar, but the stillness was not. Outside the bus window, towns passed without names she recognized. Gas stations. Empty fields. Long stretches of nothing.

The Tuskegee University campus was a beacon of rich, proud history, home to the legendary Tuskegee Airmen. MuaBana walked the grounds with a profound sense of awe, feeling the weight of the legacy she had chosen to join. This was the place where Black men had defied a prejudiced world to prove they belonged in the sky. Their photographs watched her from the walls—serious faces, pressed uniforms, eyes fixed forward. She wondered if they had felt this alone, too. She, a young Black woman from Central Africa, felt that same spirit of necessary defiance coursing through her.

She found the small, furnished room she'd rented near campus. It was clean, quiet, and utterly empty of the familiar life she'd known. There were no siblings fighting over the bathroom, no mother announcing dinner, no father's footsteps in the hallway. Even the refrigerator hummed too loudly, as if unused to silence. The silence was the loudest part of her new life.

Her first week was a frantic blur of bureaucracy: registration, medical checks, and tuition payments. The championship bonus that had felt like a King's ransom in Kananga evaporated with sickening speed under the pressure of international student fees. She had enough left for perhaps two months of rent and food, tops. The fear of failure, which had been abstract back home, was now a tangible, hungry thing.

She spent her evenings hunched over job applications, her English accent—though excellent—feeling thick and clumsy when dealing with potential employers over the phone. She practiced answers before dialing, then hung up before the phone could ring.

Loneliness settled over her like a shroud. She wanted to call her mother, to hear the soft, chaotic symphony of her family, but she knew what her mother would say: *You could have had a secure life here.*

But she also remembered the way her mother stood up for her against her father, her defiance in the face of her father putting her down. Her mother had wept for her, she had prayed for her, and had worried that she would be lonely. And MuaBana was. She was lonely; she missed her family, her brothers, the way they had encouraged her. Everything in being wanted to call her mother, to hear her voice again. To see more of the women whom she had glimpsed at that dinner.

MuaBana fought the urge, instead pulling out the laminated photo DeMuke had given her—the smiling pilot and the word: *Go.* She taped the photo above the desk, straightened it twice, then left it alone. She didn't call the number yet; she wasn't ready to admit she needed help. She was here to prove her self-sufficiency.

She was free. But freedom, she quickly realized, wasn't just a feeling; it was a grueling, expensive discipline. And discipline, she understood now, was heavier when no one was watching.

Chapter Nine:
Ground School and the Drill Sergeant

The Tuskegee Aerospace Science Program was a brutal baptism by fire. MuaBana was instantly immersed in ground school, a dizzying array of classes covering aerodynamics, meteorology, federal regulations, and navigation. The manuals were thick, printed in dense black text that assumed familiarity she did not yet have. She underlined everything. Too much, maybe. The technical language alone was a monumental barrier, requiring her to study twice as long as her American peers.

The moment she stepped into the hangar for her first flight instruction, the smell hit her first—oil, rubber, old fuel baked into concrete. The air was cooler inside, heavy with rules that did not need to be spoken. She knew she was facing a new kind of authority.

Chief Instructor Major "Rock" Davis was a retired military pilot, a man whose spine was ramrod straight and whose gaze could bore through steel. He was African American, with a salt-and-pepper buzz cut and a voice that never had to be raised to command attention. He had seen thousands of recruits and had zero tolerance for excuses. When he walked, people unconsciously moved out of his way.

His introductory speech to the new cohort was short and brutal. "You are here to learn to manage a flying machine in three dimensions. You are here to become a disciplined professional. If you are here to look good in a uniform or chase a fleeting dream, the door is right there. I will fail you. You will fail yourself. The sky will not forgive carelessness. *I* certainly won't."

Major Davis ran the program like a military academy, and he instantly singled out MuaBana.

"MuaBana Bibishbo," he barked during her first solo evaluation, making her name sound like a challenge. "You have the natural precision of a seasoned athlete. Your reflexes are sharp. But your *mind* is distracted. I see you chasing speed when you should be prioritizing safety. You are flying like a soccer star, making a break for the goal, not a pilot guiding a machine."

She swallowed. He was right. And that unsettled her more than criticism.

Later, he pulled her aside after class. "You're smart. You have the papers. You have the physical capability. But you have a burden, MuaBana."

MuaBana flinched, thinking of her father. "Sir, I left my burdens behind."

Major Davis fixed her with a hard stare, his voice solid and steady. "No, you didn't. You brought your drive to overcompensate. You're trying too hard to prove you deserve to be here, and that tension makes you rigid. It blinds you to the small, crucial details. Every time you climb into that cockpit, you have to forget the world below. You can't fly with a heavy heart, Bibishbo. And you certainly can't fly with a chip on your shoulder."

He wasn't cruel, but he wasn't soft with her either. He saw something in her and wanted the full potential in the air. So, he assigned her extra hours of simulation training, forcing her to work through endless scenarios that required methodical, calm decision-making over instinctual reaction. He wasn't just training a pilot; he was breaking down the fierce, independent warrior she had become so she could rebuild herself as a disciplined commander. Steadily, she began to understand that discipline, here, was not obedience. It was a restraint.

The pressure did not end in the hangar.

The call came late one evening, just as she was closing her books. A missed number. Then a voicemail.

"This is Mr. Thompson, airport logistics. We spoke earlier. If you're still interested in the cleaning shift, call me back."

She did not hesitate. Exhausted but validated, MuaBana stumbled toward the airport logistics office where she worked the cleaning shift, already two hours late. Her manager, a small man named Mr. Thompson, intercepted her in the hallway.

"You're cutting it close," he said, glancing at his clipboard more than at her face.

"I won't do it again," she replied, already reaching for the gloves.

The work was simple and unforgiving. Floors. Restrooms. The smell of disinfectant mixed with jet fuel clung to her clothes.

She learned the airport at night—empty gates, humming lights, planes resting like tired animals.

MuaBana started rising before dawn, spending hours in the dusty flight simulator, repeating maneuvers until her muscles ached and her brain felt saturated with data. She moved from classroom to cockpit to terminal corridor with barely enough time to eat.

Her notes grew sharper, handwriting small, rushed, and her sleep light.

She was exhausted, financially stressed, and emotionally isolated. But every morning, as the sun began to warm the hangar, she looked up at the planes and felt a sharp, undeniable surge of purpose. Fatigue did not scare her. Wasted effort did. And for her, her whole future was on the line.

*****

The next morning, she was in the campus library sorting through her notes when she came across an envelope. Thinking someone might have placed it there without her knowing, she opened it cautiously.

It was crisp and formal, in a dark envelope stamped with an unfamiliar seal. MuaBana recognized the handwriting instantly, even before she saw the name. It was the same as a letter entailing a marriage proposal. Her stomach tightened.

The words inside were few, measured, and precise.

> *Ms. MuaBana Bibishbo, I am aware of your enrollment in the Tuskegee Aerospace Science Program. I am willing to cover the cost of your tuition and program fees in full. In return, I request only a promise—your hand in marriage, to be formalized at a time of my choosing.*

MuaBana's fingers shook. The paper felt heavier than the planes she'd seen in the sky. He had found her across the ocean. He had tracked her progress. The offer was generous, almost impossible to refuse—but it came with a chain.

She folded the letter carefully and placed it in her notebook, her mind racing. She could pay her way, continue her dream without his interference—but at what cost?

She had traded one set of pressures for another. The burden of tradition had been replaced by the burden of professional competence, and this was a test she refused to fail. She visualized the planes at the simulator and reminded herself: she was here to earn her wings, not someone else's approval. The sky was the ultimate judge, and she was determined to earn its respect even if it meant paying for every inch of altitude with sweat.

Chapter Ten:
Turbulence and Sabotage

Early in the morning, before she even reached the hangar, MuaBana's stomach churned. She knew Major Davis was relentless, but this niggling feeling wasn't about the evaluation. It was a quieter, gnawing fear that had taken root in her heart since Ekonzo's letter.

She had kept her Tuskegee address private, but the thought of Etumba Ekonzo finding her room address, or of him taking her away forcibly or leveraging his influence against her, made her pulse spike. Every unfamiliar shadow in the campus hallway, every glance from a male student, felt like it might carry hidden meaning.

She arrived at her first class and froze at the sight of a small, folded envelope resting on her desk. The handwriting was crisp and familiar. Her heart thudded. Etumba's name, scribbled faintly, brought a cold sweat to her palms. She tore it open with trembling fingers:

Remember your obligations. Forget the world above.

Fear coiled in her chest. She felt the surge of anger, frustration, and helplessness all at once. This was not just a distant threat—it was a psychological weight she had to carry while trying to master flight.

Since she had not sent a reply affirming his help, he had sent her a threat. She had no qualms about it. This was a threat. The 'Or else' might as well be written there, too.

She won't give up. She stuffed the note into her bag, trying to breathe past the cold fingers tightening around her ribs. The paranoia settled in like dust, invisible but unavoidable. She glanced at every corner of the classroom, imagining eyes where there were none, calculating routes to safety even in open corridors.

As the students piled into the class, MuaBana sat in her seat, urging her thoughts to focus on something else.

*****

The mid-term flight evaluation, or "check ride," was the crucible of the Tuskegee program. It wasn't just a test of learned procedures; it was a test of command presence under stress. For MuaBana, it was a battle against her own exhaustion.

She climbed into the small, single-engine training plane with Major Davis in the co-pilot seat. His expression was a granite slab, his presence immediately amplifying the pressure in the cramped cockpit.

"Today, MuaBana," the Major stated, his voice a low, steady rumble, "we fly without a net. Any deviation from protocol, any panic, any failure to prioritize safety, and you fail the course. Begin your pre-flight checks."

MuaBana forced herself into the state of detached focus that the Major demanded. She ran through the checklist, her mind a steel trap, shutting out the memory of the night shift, the ache in her legs, and the crumpled letter from Etumba Ekonzo.

They took off, and MuaBana handled the climb-out with her usual precision, the machine responding perfectly to her athletic finesse. But the Major soon introduced chaos. He simulated a partial engine failure, demanding immediate execution of an emergency landing checklist. He barked rapid-fire air traffic control instructions, forcing her to divide her attention.

MuaBana's fatigue was almost her undoing. During a simulated stall recovery, she recovered too aggressively, a momentary reversion to the instinctual, overcompensating force that Major Davis had cautioned her against.

"Bibishbo! Control!" he snapped. "You are fighting the machine instead of *commanding* it! You're trying to out-muscle the physics, pilot. We are not on the soccer pitch!"

MuaBana took a slow, deliberate breath. *Nia's coffee, Kongolo's logic, Zuri's discipline.* She imagined the winds over the Kinshasa fields, the sunlight on the soccer pitch, the rhythmic push of her feet against the turf—her body knew precision. She visualized the problem, not the fear.

She remembered Major Davis's own words: "Tension makes you rigid. Rigid pilots break."

She didn't fight the plane. She moved with it. She led it, guided it. She corrected the altitude with a smooth, gentle touch, stabilizing the plane by precisely following the emergency procedure, not her adrenaline. For the next ten minutes, she flew with methodical, surgical calm, executing flawless maneuvers and landing procedures. She finished the ride with a perfect three-point landing, bringing the plane to a gentle, controlled stop.

Major Davis powered down the plane and sat in silence for a long moment. MuaBana held her breath.

Finally, he turned to her. "You are an infuriatingly talented pilot, Bibishbo. You are still too tense, and your focus is inconsistent. But you followed protocol when it mattered most. You learned to *command* the plane, not fight it."

He paused, a tiny flicker of approval in his eyes. "You pass. Barely. But now you need to figure out what is weighing you down. You will learn to manage it—or it will manage you. Because if I see that fatigue compromises your safety again, you're done. Go rest."

She exhaled, a single breath she didn't realize she'd been holding.

*****

Exhausted but validated, MuaBana stumbled toward the airport logistics office where she worked the cleaning shift, already two hours late. Her manager, a small, nervous man named Mr. Thompson, intercepted her in the hallway.

His face was pale. "MuaBana! You can't come in! You're fired! Effective immediately!"

MuaBana stared, dumbfounded. "Fired? Why? I always complete my shifts."

"It's a security issue," Mr. Thompson stammered, shuffling a piece of paper. "A very official-looking document arrived this morning. It concerns... your visa status and certain *irregularities* in your enrollment at the university. My head office received an anonymous, detailed report suggesting you may be using student status to circumvent labor laws."

MuaBana felt a cold knot form in her stomach. Anonymous. Detailed. This was not a coincidence. This was Etumba Ekonzo. He had followed her across the ocean. She knew it, right from the start, from that first letter.

She knew he would haunt her. His revenge was to attack her means of survival. He was trying to financially strangle her dream and force her to accept his offer.

"Who sent this report?" MuaBana demanded.

"It was routed through a law firm in New York," Thompson whispered, looking over his shoulder. "High-powered. They implied that continuing to employ you would invite a federal audit. I can't risk it, MuaBana. You have to leave."

MuaBana stood in the hallway, the victory of her flight check evaporating. Her immediate source of income was gone. The sophisticated threat was perfectly calculated: it was invisible, untraceable, and terrifyingly effective, leveraging the very anxieties of being an international student.

*****

She found a quiet spot on campus. She reached into her bag and pulled out the laminated photo DeMuke had given her weeks ago—his sister, smiling in a pilot's uniform, with the word "Go," and Nia's number scrawled on the back. She had avoided using it, wanting to prove she could manage on her own, but now there was no choice.

Hands shaking, she dialed the number. The line clicked, then a cheerful voice answered.

"MuaBana?!" Nia exclaimed, her tone warm and lively, tinged with surprise. "I've been waiting to hear from you! DeMuke told me about your dream—you really called!"

MuaBana swallowed, her throat tight. "Nia... It's bad. I... I lost my job. They cited visa issues. It has to be him—Etumba Ekonzo. This is his revenge. He's trying to corner me, cut me off, make me give in."

"This man, Ekonzo, wants to make you dependent, corner you. He's not just testing your courage; he's trying to trap you," Nia said. "He wants you to be *forced* to ask for his help. He is trying to make his cage look like a rescue boat."

"What do I do, Nia? The money is almost gone!"

Nia's voice hardened, understanding the stakes immediately. "I know exactly what's on the line, MuaBana.

"We will not let him win," Nia declared.

MuaBana let out a shaky breath. "I… I didn't want to call; I wanted to manage on my own. But… I don't have another choice."

"You did the right thing," Nia said firmly. "But we must fight smart. You are the pilot, MuaBana. You found the flight school; you found the money. Now, you use your wits. You have a soccer championship. You are brilliant."

MuaBana could hear the smile in her voice. MuaBana's shoulders eased slightly. For the first time since the first note arrived on her desk, she felt the tide shift. Nia's calm voice was like a tether to reality. A reminder that she could survive this—and even thrive.

Nia continued, "Don't let this pressure confuse your mind. You've won too much to let him shake you now. Now, you need a job that pays well, that is cash-based, and that is too small for his high-powered lawyers to track. Think, MuaBana! Where does your talent meet a need in this small town?"

MuaBana hung up, the words echoing in her mind. Her talent. Her skills. Her defiance. She had earned her wings, but now she had to fight to keep them fueled. Etumba Ekonzo had cut off her supply line, but he had underestimated her resourcefulness and the quiet, fierce determination of the community that surrounded her.

Chapter Eleven:
The Pitch and the Paycheck

Etumba Ekonzo's quiet sabotage had stripped MuaBana of her regular income, but it had also clarified her resolve. The loss stung, but it sharpened her thinking. He was attempting to control her environment, but he could not control her skills. That truth settled deep in her chest. She needed money that bypassed the university payroll and high-powered lawyers.

MuaBana knew that she needed cash, quickly and consistently. Money she could touch. Money no one could freeze or question. Money that would allow her to pursue her dreams, that would allow her to fight back.

She found her answer on the dusty, well-worn practice fields near Tuskegee's high school. She remembered how the dirt clung to her shoes. The grass was thin, stubborn, and refused to die. The field had felt honest, had driven her to be the best.

Leveraging her background—a star striker who had won the African Women's Championship—was her smartest move. It was the one thing no one could take from her. MuaBana spent a day creating and posting simple flyers near the university and local athletic centers. She taped them to corkboards and chain-link fences. Her hands moved with purpose. Her credentials spoke for themselves: "High-Intensity Soccer Striker Clinics with MuaBana Bibishbo, African Champion."

She read the words twice before walking away. They felt real. Earned.

The response was immediate. Parents of talented high school players, eager for their children to gain a competitive edge, were fascinated by the opportunity to train with an international champion. Some called out of curiosity. Others with urgency. MuaBana set her prices high; she was selling not just coaching, but expertise and discipline as well. She did not apologize for the number, even when parents and guardians approached her, hoping to barter and negotiate with her. But she knew better, had learned better. She knew that lived experience would allow her to teach with a discipline and focus that would be worth the fees. She felt in control.

She started working as a private trainer, holding intense, hour-long sessions focused on footwork, agility, and precision shooting. She ran them hard. No wasted movement. No excuses.

She trained the youth on fields far from the university to avoid Major Davis's scrutiny and minimize any appearance of a side hustle jeopardizing her studies. The cash flowed in discreetly, covering her rent and tuition payments just as they came due. Each envelope felt like air.

*****

Her reputation grew quickly. Within a week, the head coach of the local high school girls' team, impressed by the results and MuaBana's rigorous training methods, offered her a position as a paid assistant coach. The offer surprised her. It steadied her.

This provided a small, steady salary and a professional anchor in the community.

MuaBana soon found herself juggling three lives: the tireless pilot-in-training under Major Davis's brutal scrutiny, the focused college student pursuing a sustainable business administration degree (a necessary fallback she took seriously), and the demanding soccer coach building a new financial life. Each role asked something different of her. None allowed weakness.

The workload was crushing. Some mornings, she woke already tired. She would attend ground school, fly her required hours, race to the university to attend her business classes, then sprint to the high school field for practice, often coaching until the sun went down. The sky shifted colors while she worked. She then spent the rest of her evening planning the next day's lessons or studying complex aviation charts. Her eyes burned, but she kept going.

The irony was not lost on her: she had fled her family's insistence that soccer was a distraction from her studies, only to find herself relying on the game to fund her true professional pursuit. She smiled at that sometimes. Quietly to herself. Soccer was no longer a symbol of rebellion;

48

it was the engine of her freedom. It paid for fuel. It paid for hours. It paid for choice.

Soon, the financial stress began to ease, but MuaBana's physical exhaustion remained chronic. Her muscles stayed sore. Her sleep stayed thin. Yet, there was a profound difference in this fatigue: it was chosen. Each ache in her muscles, each late night spent correcting a flight plan, was a direct investment in her own future, a quiet victory over Etumba Ekonzo's attempts to control her. She owned it all. And Ekonzo will not be able to touch this.

She was teaching the local girls the same aggressive finesse she used to score her championship goals. She saw herself in them. Hungry. Determined. Watching closely. Dreaming big.

As she watched them move across the pitch, she realized she was not just funding her flight school; she was imparting the strength and defiance her parents had unknowingly cultivated in her. The lessons traveled both ways.

She was living proof that a woman's power was her own, and that one passion—the fierce discipline of the game—could sustain another—the technical mastery of the sky. She felt it every day. She was building her life one paycheck, one goal, and one flight hour at a time. The rebellion was quiet, but it was relentless.

Chapter Twelve:
The Ultimate Test

MuaBana was in the simulator, struggling to maintain altitude during a severe wind shear exercise. The enclosed cockpit felt smaller than usual. The air was stale. Plastic and metal held the heat of the day. Her movements were sluggish, her reaction time a fraction of a second too slow. She was running on three hours of sleep, her mind saturated with high school soccer drills and university notes. Her body was present, but her thoughts lagged behind, arriving late to every command.

"Altitude descending, Bibishbo! You're losing it!" Major Davis's voice crackled through the headset. The sound cut sharply, slicing through her fog. MuaBana fought the controls, heart hammering, pulling the virtual plane out of the dangerous descent. Her arms burned. Sweat slid down her spine. For a moment, instinct took over where focus failed. Major Davis didn't wait for her to finish. He cut the power to the simulator. The screens went dark. The sudden silence was worse than the shouting.

"Get out," he commanded. His voice was quiet, which MuaBana knew was far more dangerous than his shouting. Quiet meant he was done observing. Quiet meant judgment.

MuaBana climbed out of the cramped cockpit, wiping the sweat from her brow. Her legs felt heavy as they hit the concrete floor. She rolled her shoulders once, trying to wake them up.

"You are going to fail," Major Davis stated, leaning against the cold metal casing of the simulator. The chill of it contrasted sharply with her heat. "You passed the check ride because you had one moment of clarity.

Now, you are running on fumes. You look like a cleaning crew casualty, Bibishbo.”

MuaBana flinched, not at the insult, but at the accuracy. The Major had known about her previous job. He knew about her new one, too. Nothing escaped him. “I am handling my responsibilities, Major.”

The words sounded thin, even to her.

“No, you are juggling chainsaws,” he countered, crossing his arms. He looked at her the way pilots looked at storms—without emotion, only calculation. “I saw your flyers at the high school. You’re an assistant coach, a private trainer, a full-time student, and a pilot-in-training. You are trying to command the sky while running two businesses on the ground. You cannot do both, MuaBana. The human body does not defy physics.”

The phrase landed hard. Physics. Limits. Gravity. Things she respected, because they were honest.

He handed her a stark, official letter. The paper felt heavier than it should have. “This is a notification from the school registrar. We are required to inform all flight candidates of their Final Practical Exam date. You have six weeks. Six weeks to prove you are ready for your wings.”

MuaBana’s fingers shook as she took the paper. She forced them still. The date felt monumental, the final boundary between her past and her future. Everything she had survived pressed in at once—home, exile, hunger, resistance.

“Six weeks of focused, relentless study,” the Major continued. “No distractions. No fatigue. We need you sharp. The plane doesn’t care about your student loans, Bibishbo. It cares that you are rested enough to pull out of a spin.”

She pictured the nose dropping. The horizon tilted a second too late. The consequences were not theoretical. He paused, letting the weight of the exam date sink in. The room hummed softly. Somewhere outside, another engine started.

“You have two choices, MuaBana. You either resign from every single outside job today and dedicate these six weeks to the sky, or I will officially recommend your expulsion from the program due to chronic and dangerous fatigue. If you fail this exam because you are coaching a soccer team, you will not only lose your dream, but you will also waste the entire amount you’ve already paid. Choose, MuaBana. The money, or the wings.”

The words stayed with her long after he stopped speaking.

Money, or the wings.

She stood there, the paper tight in her hand, and felt the familiar pull of survival. The voice that had kept her fed. Sheltered. Moving.

But another voice rose beneath it. Quieter. Steadier. The one that had always pointed upward.

She thought of the field at dusk. The way she had trained them in the field. The lessons taught and learned. The weight of cash in her pocket. Necessary. Temporary. She thought of the sky. Endless. Unforgiving. Honest. She knew this choice would hurt no matter what. But one path ended here. The other did not. Her future depended on it. Not letting fatigue win. Not letting fear win. Not letting anyone else decide how high she was allowed to go.

She folded the letter carefully.

*****

MuaBana walked out of the hangar and into the afternoon sun, the letter a furnace in her hand. The heat hit her face immediately, sharp and unrelenting, as if the sky itself had stepped forward to test her resolve. The wide concrete apron shimmered, warped by rising heat, and the smell of fuel and hot metal clung to the air.

The ultimatum was clear: success in the air meant ruin on the ground. If she quit coaching, the money she needed for the final tuition payment and her living expenses would vanish. There was no polite way to soften it, no hopeful arithmetic that could make the numbers bend. Etumba Ekonzo's sabotage had worked perfectly; he had eliminated her previous income stream, leaving her reliant on a job the Major would now force her to abandon.

The thought tightened her chest—not rage, not surprise, but a bitter recognition of how thoroughly her options had been narrowed.

She called Nia from a quiet corner of the campus. The bench was sun-warmed, the paint peeling at the edges, its metal legs half-buried in dust. Students passed nearby, laughing, careless, their conversations floating past her like another language she no longer spoke.

"He's right, MuaBana," Nia said gently after hearing the Major's threat. "You must choose the wings. Six weeks is nothing. But what about the final tuition payment?"

"I don't have it," MuaBana admitted, the words tasting like ash. Saying them aloud made the truth heavier, more final, as if the air itself thickened around her mouth. "I needed those six weeks of coaching to get the cash. I'm short almost five hundred dollars."

"Five hundred dollars," Nia repeated. "A fortune when you don't have it. We will think. But you must quit those jobs now. You must send the Major a resignation letter for the coaching post tonight."

There was no judgment in Nia's voice, only certainty—the kind that came from someone who had survived by choosing necessity over comfort again and again.

MuaBana hung up and looked at the date on the exam notice. Six weeks. The number stared back at her, neat and unforgiving, ink pressed firmly into the paper like a verdict. Six weeks to unlearn exhaustion. Six weeks to become precise again. It was a terrifying, exhilarating countdown. She had to believe that the ingenuity that got her this far could find a solution for the last five hundred dollars. She had crossed borders with less. She had survived on smaller margins. Still, this felt different—closer, sharper, less abstract.

She sent a terse email resigning from the high school assistant coach position and texting her private clients that she had to cancel the clinics. Her fingers hesitated only once over the keyboard before moving quickly, efficiently, as if speed might dull the pain. She did not explain. She did not apologize. She simply closed the door. The money stopped instantly, but the immediate, powerful wave of relief was astonishing.

It moved through her like clean water, washing away the constant buzz in her head, the background panic she had learned to mistake for normal life. She was lighter, clearer, her mind already focusing on the complex equations of air density and flight planning. Lift, drag, wind correction—concepts that demanded respect, not desperation.

She spent the next three days living and breathing aviation, sleeping seven full hours, and working on her flight manuals until her eyes blurred with knowledge instead of fatigue. She woke before dawn without dread, her body finally aligned with purpose. The ache in her shoulders softened. Her hands steadied. Each page she turned felt like reclaiming a piece of herself that exhaustion had stolen.

The Major noticed the change immediately, a grudging nod replacing his usual scowl. It was not praise, but it was recognition—and in that space, it meant everything.

But the financial pressure remained. She was living on the few groceries she had left, rationing her meager remaining cash. Rice stretched across meals. Bread was measured, not eaten freely. She learned the exact cost of hunger—not starvation, but the persistent awareness of lack that sharpened every decision. The threat of Etumba Ekonzo and the quiet fear of her father had been replaced by a more immediate enemy: the ticking clock of the Final Practical Exam and the stark balance sheet of her bank account. One danger had receded, replaced by another that was colder, quieter, and entirely unforgiving.

She had earned her right to study, but the question remained: could she earn her right to stay?

The sky did not answer. It waited—vast, patient, and indifferent— demanding only that she arrive prepared, honest, and whole.

Chapter Thirteen:
The Golden Goal

With the threat of expulsion looming and the final exam date fixed, MuaBana had no time for gradual savings. She needed the final five hundred dollars—the difference between earning her wings and abandoning her life.

The number followed her everywhere, hovering behind her thoughts like a second shadow. Five hundred dollars was no longer abstract currency; it was fuel, rent, tuition, dignity. It was the narrow bridge between the person she had fought to become and the version of herself the world seemed determined to pull her back into.

Three days into her focused study, Nia came to MuaBana with a proposition, her eyes alight with the thrill of a secret plan. It was late—well past midnight—and the campus had fallen into its thin, restless sleep. The air inside the small room was stale with coffee and old paper, the desk cluttered with manuals, handwritten notes, and a half-eaten protein bar gone soft at the edges.

"There's a tournament," Nia whispered, huddling over MuaBana's desk in the small hours of the morning. Her voice dropped instinctively, as if the walls themselves might disapprove. "A local, underground 5-v-5 futsal league in a warehouse district in Montgomery. They call it 'The Gauntlet.' High entry fee, but the winner takes home seven hundred dollars cash. Tax-free. No paperwork. It's fast, brutal, and they play only on Saturday nights."

MuaBana's breath hitched. Her hand stilled over the page she'd been reading, the numbers blurring into meaninglessness. A single burst of risk could solve everything. Futsal—a faster, smaller-scale version of soccer—demanded extreme technical skill, agility, and precision. Her strengths.

The game lived in her muscles, in memory, in instinct. It was the language her body spoke before her mind learned caution.

"When is the final?" MuaBana asked, tracing the numbers on her tuition bill. Her fingertip lingered on the total, as if pressure alone might make it shrink.

"This Saturday. You'd have to play three matches in one night. It starts at ten and ends at two in the morning. You'd be back by dawn."

The scheduling was tight, bordering on insane. She'd be flying Sunday morning, and Major Davis would notice even a flicker of fatigue. He always did. Fatigue showed itself in the smallest betrayals—a delayed correction, a shallow breath, a hesitation where certainty should live. But the money was non-negotiable. It was the only way. There were no safe options left, only necessary ones.

MuaBana agreed. She didn't dramatize it, didn't weigh it aloud. The decision settled in her chest with the calm inevitability of gravity. Nia, using the small community network, quietly found MuaBana a team—a group of fiercely talented, street-smart women who respected MuaBana's championship pedigree and didn't ask questions about her civilian life. They didn't need her story. They only needed to know she could deliver when it mattered.

*****

Saturday night felt like stepping back into her old life, but with the pressure amplified tenfold. The drive itself felt like a crossing—out of order, out of regulation, into something raw and unsanctioned. The warehouse district sat low and wide under buzzing streetlights, concrete sweating heat even after dark. The warehouse was stiflingly hot, filled with the roar of the crowd, the smell of sweat, and the sharp, exciting echo of the ball against the floorboards.

Every sound bounced—shouts, whistles, curses, laughter—layering into a restless, electric hum.

MuaBana stepped onto the court, wearing borrowed shoes and a plain jersey. The shoes pinched slightly at the toes, unfamiliar, but she welcomed the discomfort. It anchored her. Reminded her she wasn't here for comfort. She didn't use her real name. Here, she was just "Striker."

A role, not a history. A function, not a liability.

The first two matches were grueling, testing her lungs and her long-neglected street reflexes. The pace was relentless—no room to coast, no time to recover. Sweat slicked her skin almost immediately, her breath burning sharp and fast in her chest. Her teammates were skilled, but MuaBana was a force of focused chaos. She played with a controlled, desperate intensity. Every touch mattered. Every decision was compressed into instinct and timing. The field was not the turf of her childhood; it was a pressurized chamber, and she moved with the calculated, precise energy of a professional under threat.

This wasn't nostalgia. It was survival.

In the final match, against a team of larger, more aggressive opponents, MuaBana realized she wasn't just playing for the money; she was playing to prove her body was still her own. The women across from her filled the court with their size and noise, shoulders broad, movements forceful, a style built on collision rather than craft. Every shove, every clipped ankle, carried an unspoken message: endure this or step aside.

She brought the Major's lesson into the game: command, don't fight. Control was quieter than resistance, more dangerous than force. She didn't rely on brute force; she used the deceptive feints and angle-perfect shots that had defined her youth. Small movements. Half-steps. A glance in one direction and a touch in another. The kind of play that punished impatience.

With two minutes left and the score tied, the ball flew to her feet. Time seemed to compress, the roar of the crowd dulling into a low, distant pulse. She felt the court under her soles, the sweat on her back cooling as she slowed her breath. MuaBana saw the narrowest gap—the equivalent of a perfect wind correction angle—and unleashed a low, powerful shot. There was no hesitation, no second thought. The decision lived entirely in muscle memory and trust. It sliced past the defender's boot, kissed the far post, and slammed into the back of the net.

The buzzer sounded moments later. For a heartbeat, the warehouse froze—then erupted. MuaBana collapsed to her knees, not from exhaustion, but from the sudden, powerful rush of triumph. Her hands pressed to the floor, chest heaving, eyes stinging with something dangerously close to tears. Not relief. Not joy alone. Ownership.

The team celebrated, and Nia quickly ushered MuaBana away. The noise followed them like heat, voices shouting her borrowed name, hands slapping her shoulders, laughter spilling unchecked. The seven hundred dollars, a thick, clean roll of bills, was pressed into her hand. It felt like seven hundred pounds of lifted anxiety. She didn't count it. She didn't need to. The weight alone told her everything.

MuaBana returned to her apartment just as the first streaks of dawn appeared. The city was quiet in that fragile way that only existed between night labor and morning obligation. Porch lights clicked off one by one. A bus hissed somewhere in the distance. She was physically spent, her muscles aching from the unaccustomed intensity of the futsal court. Her calves throbbed with every step, her shoulders tight, fingers stiff and swollen. The kind of pain that settled deep and promised to linger.

She didn't sleep. She couldn't afford to. Rest would dull the edge she needed to keep. She spent the morning meticulously cleaning her plane, checking every rivet and panel. The ritual steadied her. Cloth over metal. Hand along the wing. Control restored through care.

When she met Major Davis for the morning flight, he looked at her sharply. His gaze lingered longer than usual, cataloging details she couldn't hide—the tightness around her eyes, the faint stiffness in her posture.

"You look like you wrestled a bear, Bibishbo," he observed, his eyes narrowed. "I warned you about fatigue."

MuaBana, fortified by the money in her pocket and the memory of the golden goal, met his gaze without flinching. Her body ached, yes—but her mind was settled, anchored, disciplined.

"I am well-rested, Major. My mind is clear. I have secured the final payment for my tuition. There are no more distractions."

She had gambled her physical readiness against her financial necessity, and she had won. It wasn't a reckless gamble. It was a calculated one— measured, contained, and finished. Her muscles might ache, but her focus was absolute. Pain was temporary. Losing her future was not.

For the next six weeks, she lived a life of monastic discipline. Sleep became sacred. Meals were fuel, nothing more. Study blocks were unbroken, her world narrowing to manuals, checklists, and flight paths. The money was wired, and the fear of expulsion banished. Etumba Ekonzo's shadow loosened its grip.

The last hurdle was the sky itself. And this time, she would meet it without compromise.

Chapter Fourteen:
The Distraction of the Ground

The Final Practical Exam was six weeks away. With the tuition money secured, MuaBana lived with ferocious discipline. Her days were stripped down to function—wake before dawn, checklist taped to the wall, meals eaten standing, movements precise and economical. There was no wasted motion, no indulgence in fatigue or doubt. She studied, flew, and coached her private clients just enough to maintain the illusion of continuity, while pouring all her new energy into the cockpit. The illusion mattered. Appearances always did. Stability was something you performed as much as something you possessed.

The fatigue was gone, replaced by a hyper-focused, almost manic intensity. Her mind moved faster than her body now, racing through airspeed calculations and failure scenarios even as she lay still at night, eyes open, listening to the hum of the campus settling into sleep.

It was this intense focus that Akil disrupted. He entered her life quietly, the way some people do—not as an interruption, but as a subtle shift in pressure.

Akil was not involved in the Aerospace Science program; he was an Architecture student at Tuskegee, specializing in restoration. He studied buildings the way she studied aircraft—not as objects, but as systems shaped by stress, time, and intention. He was tall, with a quiet, artistic demeanor, and a mind that saw pattern and structure in the chaotic world— a necessary counterpoint to MuaBana's own precision.

He was one of the students in Nia's small circle, and while MuaBana had always kept him at arm's length, out of habit more than suspicion, he had a subtle way of noticing her tension. The way her jaw stayed clenched long after conversations ended. The way her fingers tapped invisible rhythms against her thigh, as if calibrating something only she could see.

One evening, after a grueling ten-hour day, MuaBana showed up late to Nia's informal dinner. The house was already warm with conversation and the smell of cooked onions, spice blooming in the air. Laughter spilled out through open windows, careless and unmeasured. MuaBana was agitated, having spent the afternoon failing to master a complex high-altitude wind correction.

"You look like you're about to fight the wind itself," Akil observed, handing her a plate of food.

"I am," MuaBana snapped, irritated by his casual calmness. The food was still steaming, an unfamiliar comfort she hadn't earned yet. "It's physics, not philosophy. I have six weeks. There is no room for error."

"There is always room for life," Akil countered gently. His voice didn't rise to meet hers. It didn't retreat either. "You can't command the sky if you don't remember what you're fighting for down here."

He wasn't wrong. That was the problem. Her life had become a sterile equation. Inputs and outputs. Rest and performance. Risk and reward. Even her victories were stripped of joy, reduced to checkmarks on a page. Akil offered her an escape not into reckless partying, but into contemplation. He took her to quiet, forgotten corners of the historic campus, showing her the legacy of the structures and the sheer discipline required to make a building last—the same kind of discipline she needed to make her career last.

They walked beneath aging brick facades and shadowed colonnades, places where the weight of history pressed gently rather than crushed. He spoke of load-bearing walls and stress fractures, of how beauty survived not by resisting pressure, but by distributing it.

MuaBana listened more than she spoke. For once, she did not feel the need to prove anything. Akil saw her passion, but he also saw her loneliness. He noticed how she scanned rooms instinctively, how silence unsettled her more than noise. He made her laugh, pulling her out of the cycle of anxiety and performance. The laughter surprised her every time—short bursts at first, then fuller, unguarded. It felt like oxygen.

He was the soft landing she never allowed herself. He was the opposite of the high-stakes risk she loved; he was quiet, steady comfort.

Their conversations stretched longer than intended. Walks turned into hours. Silence became shared rather than endured. Their friendship deepened quickly into a passionate, necessary escape. It was not planned. It was not strategic. It was a failure of discipline she recognized even as she surrendered to it. For the first time since she left Kananga, MuaBana was not defiant or disciplined; she was simply present. Her body remembered how to rest without collapsing. Her mind loosened its grip on outcomes.

In Akil's company, she was safe from her father's disapproval, Etumba's manipulation, and Major Davis's unforgiving standards. She didn't have to be a champion or a pilot; she was just MuaBana. A woman sitting on warm steps at dusk, listening to someone explain why old buildings deserved patience.

The whirlwind of their connection became her only release, a reckless indulgence she knew she couldn't sustain but couldn't bring herself to stop. Somewhere beneath the calm, a warning stirred. The ground had always been dangerous for her—not because it lacked meaning, but because it tempted her to stay.

*****

The blissful distraction ended abruptly three weeks before her final exam. MuaBana woke up one morning with a crushing wave of nausea, the kind that had nothing to do with turbulence.

It came in pulses, rolling through her body with a heaviness that pinned her to the mattress. Her mouth filled with bitterness. Her hands shook as she sat up, the room tilting in a way no simulator had ever prepared her for.

The truth, when she faced it, hit her with the force of an uncommanded stall.

She was pregnant.

The word sat in her chest like foreign metal. Dense. Cold. Unmovable. The confirmation from the campus clinic was a white, sterile piece of paper that felt heavier than the entire airframe of the trainer plane. The date of conception, she quickly calculated, placed the beginning of her pregnancy right around the period when she was most exhausted, most financially desperate, and most focused on the futsal league and Akil's distraction. The math was merciless. No room for interpretation. No margin for error.

The consequence of a moment of carelessness was massive, life-altering, and perfectly timed to destroy her future. She thought of the nights she had ignored the quiet warnings of her body. In the mornings, she had swallowed fatigue like medicine. The evenings she had allowed herself, just once, to be human.

The Major had warned her about the consequences of distraction; he hadn't prepared her for this. No checklist accounted for this failure mode. No emergency procedure existed for a life rerouted from the inside out.

A pregnant woman could not complete the rigorous final phase of training. The FAA requirements alone would ground her immediately. Medical clearance would be revoked before she could even argue. The sky would close itself to her without debate. She was six weeks from her license, six weeks from her goal, and now she was facing a mandatory, indefinite delay that would cost her not just the license, but potentially her entire scholarship.

Six weeks. The number mocked her now. Once a countdown. Now a wall.

Her entire quiet rebellion—the escape, the soccer, the defiance of her father—had been for nothing. Every mile she had run. Every hour she had studied. Every risk she had calculated—all of it collapsed into this single, unplanned variable. She had left her family to avoid the obligation of an arranged marriage, only to create an obligation that was far more profound and inescapable.

In her culture, pregnancy was not neutral. It was not private. It was a declaration. A sentence passed by the body itself. She was now facing the truth: she had not escaped the burden of a predetermined life; she had simply authored a new, more difficult one. One that would not wait for her readiness. One that demanded sacrifice immediately, without negotiation.

MuaBana locked the door to her room, the accepted flight plan for her life now torn to shreds. The room felt smaller with the door closed. The air was stale. The walls were too close, as if they knew. Everything suffocated her.

She was grounded. Not metaphorically. Literally. Permanently, for now. And she was utterly alone in the face of this catastrophic new reality.

She sat on the edge of the bed for a long time, hands folded in her lap, staring at nothing. The sounds of campus life drifted in through the window—footsteps, laughter, a distant engine starting. The world moved forward without hesitation.

Her body, meanwhile, had quietly made a decision without consulting her ambition. She pressed a palm against her stomach, not in tenderness, but in disbelief. This small, unseen thing had already altered the trajectory of everything she had built.

Her thoughts spiraled, sharp and unkind. Akil's face surfaced, uninvited. Not as comfort, but as a consequence. The softness she had allowed. The nights she had mistaken safety for permanence. She did not hate him. That would have been easier. What she felt instead was a hollow kind of clarity. This was not betrayal. This was mathematics. Cause and effect.

She thought of her father. The way disappointment traveled silently through bloodlines. She imagined the phone call that would never happen, the silence that would replace it instead. Shame crept in, unwelcome but familiar. Not because she was pregnant—but because she had failed to control the narrative of her own life. Control had always been her shield. Now it was gone.

Time passed strangely. Minutes stretched. Her breathing slowed. The nausea returned in waves, gentler now, as if testing her. She did not cry. There would be time for that later. Or maybe there wouldn't.

What she felt was something colder. A recalibration. A forced descent.

She knew, with a pilot's certainty, that some losses could not be recovered mid-flight. Some emergencies demanded landing, whether you were ready or not. The sky had been her refuge. Now it was the thing she might lose entirely.

MuaBana lay back on the bed and stared at the ceiling. For the first time since leaving home, she did not know what the next correct action was. There was no checklist for this moment. Only the weight of consequence, and the silence that followed it.

Chapter Fifteen:
The Clock and the Cockpit

MuaBana did not confront Akil. She did not seek counsel from Nia. She did not even allow herself the luxury of thinking about them for long, letting the sound of their voices drift in and out like distant radio chatter. Instead, she retreated into the same shell of fierce, isolated discipline that had marked her first few weeks in Tuskegee. Her apartment became a fortress of papers, charts, and flight manuals stacked in precise columns. The hum of the ceiling fan, the scent of coffee and worn leather, the dim evening light cast long shadows across the room. The knowledge of the pregnancy was a cold, hard secret that she locked away, turning her six remaining weeks into a solitary, desperate mission.

No one could know. Not Akil. Not Nia. Not even herself fully, in moments when exhaustion blurred her clarity. The secret rested heavily in her chest, pressing against her ribs like the pressure in a cabin during a climb.

Her pregnancy, mercifully, offered no physical discomfort. The nausea had passed quickly, and the physical changes were subtle—a slight softening of her usually rock-hard abdomen, easily concealed beneath the loose flight uniform.

She noticed the gentle curve only in the privacy of her own apartment, reflected in the tall mirror beside her dresser, or in the rare moments when she caught herself in the cockpit window. Her reflection was both familiar and strange, like seeing a familiar airfield altered by storm clouds.

Her soccer training, ironically, helped mask the early changes. Her legs, strong and practiced, carried her with the same precision they had for years, as though every muscle remembered its old rhythm and refused to betray her.

Her body, though, was undergoing a deep, biological shift, and MuaBana knew the reprieve was temporary. She could feel it in the subtle fatigue that lingered behind her shoulder blades, in the faint, almost imperceptible flutter in her stomach when she changed altitude quickly. Every adjustment in the simulator, every flight maneuver, felt slightly different, requiring more attention, more care.

She had to secure her pilot's license—her financial freedom, her professional legitimacy, her entire future—before the pregnancy forced her to stop. The stakes were no longer abstract; they were cellular. They had become something that lived inside her, demanding vigilance and precision at every breath.

She viewed the final exam not just as a professional test, but as a betrayal of her body. The Major's scrutiny became a terrifying lens. He had the eyes of a hawk and the patience of a sculptor, noticing the tiniest tremor in her hands, the smallest hitch in her exhalation, the almost imperceptible hesitation in her fingers as she flipped switches. Every subtle hitch in her breath, every moment of fatigue, could betray her secret and lead to instant expulsion. The stakes pressed down on her like a canopy of storm clouds just before the horizon line disappears.

She intensified her studying, relying on pure adrenaline and willpower. Late nights blurred into early mornings, the pages of textbooks smeared with pencil marks and highlighted sections, coffee cooling into bitterness at her side. She studied weather patterns, flight regulations, emergency procedures, and aerodynamics with the meticulous obsession of someone staring down a deadline that could not be postponed.

She had gambled her last money; now, she was gambling her most precious resource: time.

*****

Major Davis was impressed by her renewed focus. He noticed the palpable change after she cut her side jobs—the sharp intelligence returned to her eyes, and her execution of complex procedures was flawless. She moved with the quiet efficiency of someone who had removed every non-essential variable from her orbit, someone who understood that failure was a luxury she could no longer afford.

But the Major was a seasoned observer, trained to notice the smallest deviation in a pilot's presence. He had flown under more extreme conditions than any of the trainees would face in their careers, and yet he remained vigilant for those almost invisible cracks—the fatigue in a shoulder, the tension in a jaw, the hesitation before a crucial decision.

"Bibishbo," he said one afternoon during a review of her weather chart analysis, the afternoon sun falling through the hangar windows, throwing long stripes across the polished concrete, "you are flying like you have a deadline. Your technique is perfect, but your mind is too urgent. You are anticipating failure, not success. The sky does not reward desperation."

MuaBana maintained a careful facade of calm. She nodded minutely, letting the words wash over her without revealing the undercurrent of panic that thrummed in her veins like a hidden tachometer. "My tuition is paid, Major. My distractions are gone. My only deadline is the final exam."

"Good," he grunted, unconvinced. "Because the examiner doesn't care about your reasons. He only cares about your command."

He let the words hang in the thick, humid air of the hangar, punctuated by the faint scent of aviation fuel and warm metal.

The closer the exam date came, the more MuaBana had to fight the quiet exhaustion that seemed to pool in her muscles, a new kind of fatigue that sleep barely touched. It was the exhaustion that came from knowing a secret, from carrying it alone, and from watching time tick down relentlessly. Her joints ached slightly, her wrists tingled after long hours of manipulating flight controls, and even her breathing seemed to require effort she hadn't noticed before. She wore a heavy jacket during ground classes, sweating under the humid Alabama sun to conceal the slight, rounding change in her figure. Every glance from a fellow student, every casual comment from instructors, felt like a potential exposure.

She also had to face Akil. The weight of his absence pressed on her unexpectedly in quiet moments—the small table at Nia's apartment suddenly felt emptier, his laughter absent from the hallways of the campus, the gentle way he had noticed the angle of her shoulders now missing.

She had pulled away abruptly, offering no explanation, claiming relentless focus on the exam. Akil, hurt and confused, tried to talk to her once, intercepting her on the way to the hangar.

"MuaBana, you can't just cut people out," he pleaded, reaching for her arm. His hand lingered for a moment, warm and alive against her uniform, and she felt the temptation of normality, of connection, stab through her concentration. "This isn't just about the license, is it? What's going on?"

MuaBana looked at his face—the last link to a moment of weakness, a life she now had to violently postpone. She saw the concern in his eyes, the subtle worry etched in the fine lines at the corners, the way he had remembered the quiet details of her life she hadn't noticed herself.

She could only give him the necessary, brutal lie. "This is about the license, Akil. My future is in the sky. Anything on the ground is a distraction."

She left him standing alone, choosing the professional lie over the emotional truth. His eyes followed her, filled with a silent question she could not answer, and she felt the pang of loss but buried it beneath layers of focus and determination, the only armor she had left.

*****

The day of the final exam dawned hot and still. The sun hung low and heavy over Tuskegee, baking the tarmac in a shimmer of heat waves. The humidity pressed against MuaBana's skin, settling in the small bead of sweat at her hairline, in the crease behind her knees, in the hollow of her neck. Even the scent of jet fuel and cut grass mixed into a thick, almost suffocating perfume that reminded her she was very much on the ground, though she would soon rise above it all.

Her chest rose and fell with the sticky weight of the morning, each breath a reminder that the sky was both sanctuary and crucible. MuaBana was wearing her tightest uniform shirt, hoping the stiffness would hold her secret for just a few more hours. She tugged at the collar once, twice, smoothing the fabric over her stomach, willing the silhouette to read as discipline rather than the subtle truth of life growing inside her.

Her examiner was not Major Davis, but a severe, uniformed FAA officer named Mr. Vance—a quiet man known for his rigid adherence to protocol. He carried the air of someone who had seen every possible mistake at least twice, whose eyes missed nothing, and whose silence could weigh as heavily as any rebuke. MuaBana knew that this man would not care about her story, her struggles, her hunger for freedom. To him, she was a pilot in evaluation, nothing more, nothing less.

MuaBana performed the initial take-off and navigation perfectly. The engine had hummed a steady, familiar cadence beneath her fingertips. The vibration through the yoke grounded her thoughts and kept panic at bay.

The cotton of her gloves had stuck slightly to her palms from sweat, but she barely noticed it; all attention was on trim, angle, and instruments. Her mind, sharp and focused, cataloged the humidity, the thin thermals rising off the fields below, the erratic movements of a lone hawk she passed overhead. Every detail mattered, every subtle cue from the environment a signal to her survival. Her senses had heightened by the high stakes.

But Mr. Vance had a defining test: The Engine Stall/Fire.

It was the culmination of every drill, every sweat-soaked hour in the simulator, every memorized emergency checklist. She knew it was coming, but anticipation did nothing to ease the weight of imminent trial.

Mid-flight, over an unfamiliar stretch of rural Alabama farmland. It was a patchwork of fields of green and gold spreading like a quilt below, dotted with barns and meandering dirt roads, the air thick with the scent of recently turned soil. Mr. Vance suddenly pulled the throttle and yelled: "Simulated fire! Engine failure at cruise altitude! You have fifteen seconds to identify and initiate checklist procedures!"

The cockpit was plunged into a terrifying quiet. The sudden silence felt like the moment a drumstick lifts before a thunderous beat, like the calm breath before a storm. Her heart slammed in her chest, and a thin sheen of sweat spread across her forehead and neck, glinting in the sunlight streaming through the canopy.

MuaBana's adrenaline spiked, but beneath the fear was the cold, practiced discipline Major Davis had drilled into her. Command, don't fight. The mantra echoed in her skull, a tether keeping her tethered to reason while panic threatened to pull her into free fall.

But the sudden, crushing anxiety brought with it an unexpected physiological response: a sharp wave of nausea that threatened to overwhelm her. The pressure, the heat, the sudden pull on the controls— it was too much.

Her stomach churned violently, a tight, knotting pressure that she had no time to analyze. The taste of bile was metallic, the sweat now slick along her jawline, her fingers trembled just slightly as they hovered over the throttle. Her pulse throbbed in her temples, her lungs burned slightly from the exertion, and for the first moment, she felt the full, human vulnerability of her situation. She was not just MuaBana the pilot; she was MuaBana, fragile, secret-laden, and very alive.

She fought the urge to gag, forcing her focus back to the instrument panel. She wasn't fighting the controls, or the wind, or the Major. She was fighting her own body.

Command, don't fight!

She focused on the first step: Identify the problem. Her mind sharpened, stripping away every distracting thought: nausea, the secret growing in her belly, the judgment of Mr. Vance. Nothing mattered except procedure. Then, she applied the memory checklist with methodical calm: Fuel off, mixture cut, cabin heat off, emergency descent.

She realized the problem wasn't the engine; the problem was the panic. She had to trust the process. A small, ironic smile threatened to tug at her lips as she acknowledged the truth. Years of drilling, of focus, of repeated simulations, had taught her that control was always internal first. She inhaled deliberately, exhaled through her teeth, and centered herself in the cockpit like a calm eye at the center of a storm.

She established the best glide speed, turning the plane toward a suitable emergency field she had spotted on the map just seconds before the simulation. She brought the plane into a controlled, silent glide over the unsuspecting Alabama fields. The red-brown of plowed earth and the muted green of spring pastures spread below her, a reassuring visual grid, each line guiding her trajectory. Her stomach still fluttered, but her hands moved with precision, muscles recalling drills by memory, heartbeat syncing with engine hum.

When she finished the simulated emergency landing, she had saved the plane and the two lives on board by following the procedures exactly. Her own body trembled with exhaustion, but she did not allow herself to acknowledge it. Sweat had beaded along her temples, her uniform clung damp to her back, and her pulse thundered in her ears like a warning bell. Every nerve felt alive, stretched taut, a reminder of the cost of perfection.

Mr. Vance simply said, "We'll taxi back to the hangar now, Bibishbo."

MuaBana waited, exhausted and terrified, for the verdict.

She had flown perfectly, but had the nausea shown on her face? Had the exertion betrayed the secret she was desperate to keep?

Her hands rested lightly on the yoke, still trembling, and she felt the sticky heat of the Alabama morning, the tang of jet fuel and warm metal, and the ache of muscles that had carried her beyond ordinary limits. All of it—the panic, the focus, the fear, the secrecy—culminated in this single, taut moment. She exhaled slowly, letting herself exist in the stillness, before stepping from the cockpit into a future she had fought to claim.

Chapter Sixteen:
The Sky's Silence

MuaBana taxied the small training aircraft back to the hangar with surgical precision, her movements slow and deliberate. The morning sun reflected off the aluminum fuselage, casting a harsh, white glare that made her squint even through the shaded visor of her cap. She powered down the engine, and the sudden, heavy silence in the cockpit was almost unbearable. For a moment, all she could hear was the tick of the canopy latch cooling and the distant squawk of a red-tailed hawk circling the fields beyond the hangar. It was quiet, so complete that it made her own pulse sound deafening.

Mr. Vance, the FAA examiner, methodically clicked his pen, filling out the final boxes on his clipboard. The sound of the pen scratching against paper was sharp and almost accusatory in the heavy, still air of the hangar. MuaBana fought the urge to glance at herself in the reflective instrument panel, scanning for any sign that her secret—her condition—had betrayed her. The tiny swell under her uniform, subtle yet undeniable, was a physical reminder that the victory she was about to receive came with an invisible, unspoken weight.

MuaBana waited, her palms pressed lightly against the yoke as if holding on to some last tether to control, to calm. Every muscle in her body was taut, from the tension in her shoulders to the ache in her calves from gripping rudder pedals that had been her constant companions for weeks. The air smelled faintly of jet fuel, warm metal, and sweat—a combination that had become the scent of her life here, of sacrifice and obsession. She fought the urge to check her reflection for signs of the secret swelling beneath her uniform. The anxiety of the past three weeks—the futsal game, the Major's threats, Akil's confusion, and the constant, crushing knowledge of the baby—all compressed into this single, agonizing moment.

Mr. Vance finally closed his clipboard and turned to her. His severe expression had not softened, but there was a flicker of professional respect in his eyes.

"Bibishbo," he began, his voice dry and devoid of enthusiasm. "Your performance during the simulated emergency descent and the subsequent procedures was textbook. You maintained a high level of situational awareness, and your resource management was excellent." His gaze was piercing as he continued, "Your instincts for command are sharp, and your execution precise under pressure. Few students can reconcile panic with discipline the way you did."

He pushed the paperwork toward her. "The written test score was high. Your flight log is complete. You have successfully passed your Final Practical Examination."

MuaBana felt a rush of air leave her lungs, a silent, powerful expulsion of three years of pressure and sacrifice. Relief filled her. It was almost tangible. It settled in her chest like warm sunlight into the rigid bones of her shoulders, softening the tension she hadn't realized she'd been carrying. For a heartbeat, she allowed herself to imagine the wide, open skies again—as a space of freedom she had finally earned. Her fingers tingled as they grazed the edges of the laminated form; it felt impossibly light and impossibly heavy all at once.

She had done it. She had defied her father, defeated Etumba Ekonzo's sabotage, and outwitted Major Davis's scrutiny. She was officially a Commercial Pilot.

"Congratulations, Pilot Bibishbo," Mr. Vance said, extending a hand. "Welcome to the sky."

*****

The moment MuaBana received the official license card—a small, laminated piece of plastic that represented her entire future—the triumph dissolved. The joy was immediately hollowed out by the biological reality. The card felt heavier in her hand than its size warranted, a cold, flat testament to her achievement. The smooth surface reflected her face back at her: tired eyes rimmed with faint red, her lips pressed together in a forced calm, a body that had carried her through every crisis and emerged victorious.

She stood in the hangar office, the smell of jet fuel and ambition heavy in the air, but all she could feel was the small, resolute life growing inside her. She had won her freedom, but she had simultaneously created the most profound obligation of her life.

Major Davis appeared in the doorway, a rare, genuine smile on his face. "Pilot Bibishbo! You earned those wings. You flew with the focus I always knew you had. Now, take a week off. Celebrate. You've been running on empty long enough."

He walked away, leaving MuaBana alone with the new license. The hangar seemed suddenly vast and hollow, sunlight streaming in across dust motes that floated lazily in the still air. She held the card tightly between thumb and forefinger, feeling both triumph and trepidation. The fluorescent lights hummed overhead, but could not compete with the thundering pulse in her own ears, a constant reminder that the flight she had just completed was only the beginning.

She felt a strange mixture of pride and panic, a tension that twisted her stomach and made her palms clammy even in the relative stillness of the hangar office.

She hadn't been running on empty; she had been running on two lives. And the Major's final advice—to rest, to take a week off—was an ironic command that she desperately needed but couldn't afford. The minute she confessed her condition, the license would be provisional, her career path indefinitely delayed.

She was now a qualified professional, but she was also a secretly pregnant single mother. Her victory was not freedom, but a more complex, personalized kind of cage.

*****

MuaBana drove away from Moton Field, the historic training ground of the Tuskegee Airmen, feeling like a fraud. She had succeeded in her rebellion against her old life, only to create a conflict that dwarfed the old one.

The time for solitude was over. She could not postpone the truth any longer. Her priority was to use her secured professional status as leverage for the impossible conversations ahead.

First, she had to face her unborn baby's father.

MuaBana pulled up outside the quiet, historic house where Akil rented a room. The heavy, humid air of Montgomery pressed against her through the cracked window, a reminder that life outside the cockpit offered no autopilot. She got out of the car, the flight jacket feeling like a suit of armor she was about to discard. She didn't have a plan, only a terrifying necessity.

She found Akil sketching on his porch, headphones in. The faint scratch of pencil against paper paused mid-stroke as he sensed her presence, his brow furrowing before he even looked up. He looked up, his face immediately clouding with the hurt she had inflicted with her abrupt dismissal. The warm golden hour light softened the lines of his expression, yet the pain and confusion in his eyes cut through her like a sharp wind.

"I told you I needed to focus," MuaBana said, her voice strained, thick with unshed tension and fatigue from the weeks of hidden battles. She pulled the plastic license card from her pocket and tossed it onto his sketchpad. It landed with a light clink, spinning slightly before coming to rest over the delicate outline of a building he'd been drawing. "I got it. I passed. I'm a pilot."

Akil looked at the card, then back up at her, waiting.

MuaBana took a deep, steadying breath, one she couldn't afford to lose. Her chest rose and fell slowly, the humid air filling her lungs like a warning, a reminder that some battles could not be flown with instruments or checklists. The discipline she had learned in the cockpit was useless here. She reached down and placed her hand over her lower abdomen. She felt the small, persistent weight that made every heartbeat sharper, every breath heavier, and stated the truth plainly, without apology or explanation.

"I need to talk to you. I'm pregnant. And it's yours."

The sound of his pencil clattering onto the floor was the last noise before the silence returned, heavier and more devastating than any Major Davis had commanded in the cockpit. It was oppressive, folding around them like the heavy Alabama air at sunset. Every shadow seemed to stretch longer, every creak of the porch a reminder of the enormity of the moment.

The rebellion was finally over, but the consequences were just beginning.

Chapter Seventeen:
Akil's Choice

Akil stared at the license card, then at MuaBana's resolute, exhausted face. The card felt absurdly small for what it carried, a thin rectangle heavy with consequence. The silence stretched, thick with accusation and shock. Somewhere beyond the porch, the late afternoon insects hummed, indifferent to the moment unfolding. MuaBana held her breath, prepared for confusion, denial, or anger.

Finally, Akil stood, his gaze sweeping across her figure, suddenly seeing the subtle concealment of her jacket and the deep lines of strain around her eyes. Details he had missed before now assembled themselves into something undeniable.

"You knew," he said, his voice quiet and wounded. "You knew this was happening, and you still pushed me away. You still went through that exam, gambling with our child's safety, without saying a single word."

"I had to," MuaBana insisted, the familiar heat of defensive determination rising in her chest. Her fingers curled into her palms, as if anchoring herself. "I had six weeks. If I told the Major, if I told anyone, they would ground me instantly. The fees would not be refunded, and the scholarship would be lost. I had to secure the license first. I needed the leverage."

Akil ran a hand over his face, sinking onto the porch step. The wood creaked under his weight, a small sound that broke something open in him. "Leverage. MuaBana, this isn't a business deal. This is a life. Our life."

She sat beside him, the cold, analytical part of her mind taking over. "I know. And I made a mistake, Akil. But a mistake doesn't have to be a disaster. I have my wings now. I have the foundation to support this child, and myself, on *my* terms, not Etumba Ekonzo's, and not my father's."

She looked at him, her vulnerability showing only in her eyes. Her voice stayed steady, but her breath did not. "This child is mine. I will not compromise my career. I will work, I will hire care, and I will fly. But I need to know: what is your choice? I am not asking you to marry me, or even stay here. But I need to know if you are a father who will be involved, or a memory I have to leave behind."

Akil looked at the license card, the tiny script of her name and qualification. He traced the letters with his eyes, imagining the nights she must have endured alone to earn them. He saw the strength required to achieve that, and the terrifying fear beneath it.

"I can't believe you hid this," he whispered, shaking his head. His disappointment was real, but it no longer stood alone. "But I can't leave you. I can't leave my child."

He took her hands, his touch warm and stabilizing. It was the first time since she arrived that she allowed herself to lean into it. "I'm in my final year. I can finish here. I will be a father, MuaBana. I won't disappear. I'll support you, but you need to stop fighting alone. You need to tell your family."

Akil's acceptance was a powerful relief, lifting a significant portion of the crushing, solitary burden. For the first time since the exam, since the silence, she felt the weight shift from her chest to the ground beneath her feet. But the second, and far more terrifying, burden remained.

Chapter Eighteen:
The New Burden

MuaBana spent a day composing the call in her head. She rehearsed courage the way she once rehearsed emergency checklists—methodical, precise, hoping preparation could soften the impact. She had faced down Major Davis, outmaneuvered a high-powered corporate saboteur, and passed the FAA exam. But telling her father that she was pregnant out of wedlock, two years after running away to pursue a career he had forbidden, was the hardest confrontation of her life.

This wasn't a test she could pass with skill alone.

She called the family's landline, knowing her mother would answer first. The familiar ring grounded her and unsettled her at the same time.

"Maman," MuaBana said, her voice cracking for the first time in months. "I have news. I did it. I got my pilot's license."

Maman Bibishbo's voice exploded with relief and pride. "MuaBana! My daughter! My God, we knew you could do it! Your brothers are here— they've been following the Tuskegee news online! We are so proud!"

The pure, unconditional joy from her mother was almost too much to bear. It provided the strength MuaBana needed for the second piece of news. But it also struck her with sudden guilt—this joy she was about to fracture.

"Maman... there is something else. Something difficult. I'm pregnant. And the father is a man here in Tuskegee. I am not married."

The line went silent. The celebration, the rush of familial warmth, vanished instantly. MuaBana stared at the wall, suddenly aware of how alone she was in that small room.

MuaBana heard her mother inhale sharply, then cover the receiver to muffle a panicked gasp. After a long moment, Maman Bibishbo spoke, her voice strained and thin. "Your father is here, MuaBana. I have to tell him."

Papa MukandaMoyo took the phone. His voice, when it came, was not the roar of disappointment MuaBana expected, but a cold, deadly, measured tone that was far worse.

"You have chosen your path," he said, the words heavy with finality. "You left this family to pursue your ambition. We accepted that. We accepted the risk. But this... this is not ambition. This is shameful. You have soiled your reputation, MuaBana, and brought dishonor to a professional qualification that should have been your shield."

MuaBana felt tears stinging her eyes. She forced herself to remain still, refusing the instinct to apologize for existing. "Papa, I am a pilot. I am capable. I will support this child. I will not stop flying."

"A woman who sacrifices her family's name for a temporary indiscretion and a piece of paper is a foolish woman," he thundered, his control finally breaking. "You threw away security, you threw away the opportunity of Etumba Ekonzo, and now you have created a new burden that will forever ground you. You are on your own, MuaBana. You will not return to this house until you have proven that you can be both a mother and a responsible professional, without any aid from the wealth you so easily scorned."

His words landed with weight, but not surprise. Some part of her had always known love, in his world, was conditional on obedience.

He didn't disown her, but he gave her a new ultimatum: Prove your self-sufficiency entirely.

Just as the line went dead, MuaBana's phone rang instantly. It was Mpetu, her older brother, speaking for the siblings.

"Don't listen to him, Mua," Mpetu said, his voice firm and strong. "He's hurt, not right. He is grieving the life he planned for you."

"But he's right, Mpetu. This is going to make everything harder." She pressed her hand to her stomach, already negotiating futures in her mind.

"Yes," Mpetu agreed. "But you're not Etumba Ekonzo's property, and you are not alone. Maman is upset, but she is already planning. She said to tell you: You have your wings. We will make sure you keep them."

Mpetu explained that the siblings—including him, Kongolo, and KankoloNkonko—had banded together. They couldn't pay her fees, obeying their father's strict command against financial aid. But they could provide a practical solution.

"We will pool our resources, Mua, and buy your maternity flight suits and pay for the childcare deposit near the Tuskegee campus. We won't pay for your tuition or rent, but we will make sure you have the tools you need to stay in the air. The final test is for Papa, Mua: you have to prove you can hold both lives together. You have to fly."

MuaBana hung up, the tears finally falling—not from shame, but from the realization of the powerful, unconditional love that transcended her father's traditional demands. She had been raised to believe strength came from hierarchy. Instead, it came from solidarity. Her rebellion had cost her the approval of her patriarch, but it had earned her the unbreakable support of her peers. For the first time, she understood that family could bend without breaking. She was a licensed pilot, a mother-to-be, and she was going to have to prove herself all over again.

Chapter Nineteen:
The Captain's Return

Eighteen months after MuaBana received her license, her life was a symphony of relentless logistics and soaring success. She had taken a short, necessary pause after the birth of her son, Disanka (meaning "joy" in Tshiluba), leaning heavily on Akil, Nia, and the financial assistance from her siblings for childcare. She completed her instructor certifications and quickly secured a position as a First Officer for a regional cargo transport company flying out of Atlanta, specializing in freight routes across the Southeast.

Her uniform was now slightly tailored to accommodate her post-pregnancy body, and she wore her new gold wings with the quiet confidence of someone who had fought for every rivet.

Her ultimate high-stakes career moment came on her first major commercial transport flight: a nighttime run carrying critical medical supplies from Atlanta to the Caribbean. The flight was plagued by unforecast severe thunderstorms over the Atlantic. As she studied the weather brief, a familiar calm settled in—not hope, not fear, just responsibility.

MuaBana, in the left seat, was forced to take command. The cockpit vibrated with turbulence, and her captain, a veteran named Ms. Diaz, watched her closely. The conditions were terrifying—gusts of wind shearing at the wings, lightning flashing across the radar screen. Somewhere in the noise, she became aware of her breathing and adjusted it, the way she had learned to do after Disanka's birth—slow, deliberate, present.

She also remembered long nights rocking a crying infant, learning that force never solved what patience could.

MuaBana did not panic. She did not overcompensate. She remembered Major Davis's instruction: "Command, don't fight." She used the precision and planning she'd honed on the soccer pitch and in the simulator, calmly navigating the narrow, safe corridors between the massive storm cells. Her focus was absolute, her movements minimal and effective. She was the disciplined commander, prioritizing safety and procedure over instinct.

When they finally broke through the clouds into clear air, the plane steady and the mission intact, Captain Diaz unbuckled her harness and looked at MuaBana with profound respect.

"Well done, First Officer Bibishbo," she said. "You flew that like you had something important waiting for you at the destination."

MuaBana smiled, glancing at the small, worn photo of Disanka and Akil tucked into her logbook. She touched it briefly, not for comfort, but as acknowledgment.

"I do, Captain. I have a lot waiting for me on the ground," she said, her voice firm.

Her competence was proven not just as a pilot, but as a working mother, managing the dual demands of a professional life and a child. The turbulence was a final test, and she had passed. Not by becoming someone new—but by fully inhabiting who she already was.

*****

Two years after her defiant departure, MuaBana flew back to the Congo, not as a fugitive, but as the First Officer on a chartered flight carrying relief aid into Kinshasa. The flight was expensive, but the symbolism was priceless. As the aircraft descended, she looked out over the familiar sprawl of land and felt no urge to explain herself to it. The ground did not judge—it simply received.

She dressed in her crisp uniform and carried Disanka, now a sturdy, babbling toddler, on her hip. His weight was solid, grounding—nothing like the abstract fears that had once haunted her. Akil, who had finished his degree and found a job teaching in Atlanta, waited for her in Kinshasa to connect with her family. They had learned how to stand beside one another without crowding, without diminishing.

The meeting was at her parents' house in Kananga. Her mother, Mpetu, Kongolo, and KankoloNkonko rushed forward, embracing her and cooing over Disanka, the cheers and tears a chaotic wave of love. The house felt smaller than she remembered, but warmer—filled with motion, sound, life continuing despite absence.

Then, MuaBana saw her father. He was standing in the doorway, a solid, unmoving figure, his face etched with two years of pride, confusion, and lingering resentment. He looked older, she noticed—not weaker, just marked by time and unsaid words.

MuaBana walked toward him, not with defiance, but with dignity. Each step felt deliberate, measured, as though she were crossing a runway rather than a room. She stopped before him, standing tall in her uniform, her son nestled on her hip.

"Papa," she said, her voice steady. "I have returned. I am a licensed pilot. I have my wings, and I have honored the strength you taught me." She held out her hand, not for a hug, but for a handshake, offering him the respect of one professional to another. She was not asking for permission—only recognition.

Papa Bibishbo looked at the gold wings pinned to her chest, then down at Disanka, the grandson whose existence was the source of his shame and his quiet, new joy. The child reached a curious finger toward the pilot's wings. The small gesture disrupted something rigid and long-held.

The father's strict, traditional facade finally crumbled. He didn't speak. He reached out and gently touched Disanka's head, then looked back at MuaBana's resolute face. In that moment, she saw not authority, but assessment—the careful reckoning of a man who valued outcomes above intention.

"You built this life yourself, MuaBana," he said, his voice thick with emotion. "You accepted the cost. You did not ask for our aid." He paused, looking at Akil, who stood a respectful distance away. "And you have managed your burden."

He did not apologize for his actions, but his acceptance was absolute. He pulled MuaBana into a fierce, long hug—the reconciliation not of a daughter who was forgiven, but of a peer who was respected.

She let herself be held, not as a concession, but as closure.

The family gathered around them. MuaBana looked at the chaos, the love, the sound of her son's laughter echoing through the hall. She hadn't found the easy life her father planned, but she had achieved something far greater: self-determination.

MuaBana Bibishbo had not escaped her burden; she had redefined it. She was not leaving as a fearful child, nor was she returning as a runaway. She had come home as the Captain of her own destiny. And this time, she did not need to take off to prove it.

Epilogue:
The Captain's Legacy

The decades that followed were marked not by wedding rings, but by a life richly documented in type ratings, flight hours logged, and soccer trophies earned. Muabana never married. Her choice was rooted in a hard-won, loving wisdom, making her independence an active, determined rejection of the patriarchal failures she had witnessed. Now, she commanded long-haul international routes as a seasoned Airline Captain, shuttling passengers and cargo across the continents she once desperately fled, her powerful journey a testament to the life she chose and fiercely loves.

*****

The moment MuaBana revealed her pregnancy, Akil did not become a partner; he became a ghost. He maintained a false front of support only until MuaBana received her license. As the reality of fatherhood set in, the promise he'd made on the porch dissolved. Akil disappeared entirely, leaving Tuskegee and cutting off all contact, unable to face the responsibility that clashed with his own ambitions.

MuaBana accepted his departure with a cold case. Her ultimate security was never tied to his presence; she had secured her pilot's license for herself and her son, Disanka. She changed Disanka's surname to her mother's maiden name, severing the link to the man who chose ambition over obligation.

A few years later, MuaBana met Elias, a pilot with another carrier. Their relationship resulted in the birth of the twin boys, Mpetu and

87

Kongolo. However, MuaBana soon discovered Elias was married and had concealed the truth from her entirely.

The betrayal was immediate and absolute. It reinforced her hardest lesson: she didn't need a partner for fulfillment, only for conception. The two men in her life had failed the basic test of honesty and commitment. She ended the relationship with Elias instantly, drawing a definitive line. She would be the sole, unwavering Captain of her own life and her children's futures. She raised her three sons as a proud, intentional single mother, politely declining every subsequent suitor.

*****

The sprawl of MuaBana's home in Peachtree City, Georgia, was an architectural contradiction: grand, yet deliberately unpolished. It was a space designed for landing, not takeoff—a home built on love and jet fuel. Inside, the energy was less a smooth glide path and more a controlled sonic boom: loud, chaotic, and filled with the familiar clamor she craved after days spent in the sterile solitude of the sky.

She could be anywhere—London, Dubai, Rio—but the relentless, rhythmic clamor of her three boys always pulled her back. The three boys—Disanka, Mpetu, and Kongolo—were a force of nature, a midfield trio in life as on the pitch, and their noise was a comforting, necessary anchor. MuaBana, however, was not just their mother. She was MuaBana, the international champion—the legend who'd redefined what a woman could do in a cockpit—and she was their primary coach.

She drove them to practice not in a minivan, but in a black Range Rover that smelled perpetually of freshly polished leather and damp, grassy cleats. As the car pulled up to the training grounds, she didn't give them a motivational cheer; she gave them an operational briefing.

"The field," she would say, her eyes already scanning the horizon as if looking for cloud cover, "is merely a larger, grassier cockpit."

She trained them for precision and command, teaching them to see the field as she saw the instrument panel—an environment demanding disciplined anticipation. Power, she taught, was cheap; everyone could kick hard. But like a pilot managing crosswinds during a difficult approach, they had to manage the variables. They learned that a burst of power was useless without control; it was an energy expenditure that had to be justified by an expected outcome.

They stepped onto the practice pitch, the bright green turf absorbing the late afternoon sun. Disanka, the eldest and the most aggressive, immediately began winding up for a hard shot on an empty goal.

"Negative," MuaBana's voice cut across the field, sharp and immediate, like a warning chime in the cockpit. Disanka froze, the ball half-kicked.

"Disanka, what is the mission objective?" she asked, not raising her voice, yet commanding attention.

Disanka sighed, retrieving the ball. "To score, Mama."

"Incorrect. The immediate mission objective is controlled velocity. Show me the $45 approach angle. Mpetu, Kongolo, watch his sightlines."

Mpetu, the second, moved in close, tracking Disanka's posture. Disanka took a breath, adjusted his run-up, and struck the ball. Instead of a blazing line drive, it was a perfectly arcing shot that kissed the crossbar and dropped into the net. It was slower, but utterly inescapable.

"Precision," MuaBana nodded, a flicker of approval in her eyes. "That arc was repeatable. That goal was not luck; it was a calibrated outcome. We don't just fly high; we land exactly where we intend to."

She then turned her attention to Kongolo, the youngest, who was already running a complex zigzag pattern with the ball glued to his foot. "Kongolo, your lateral stability is excellent. But remember the wind-shear protocol. Watch the opposing midfield—they are not obstacles, they are turbulent variables. Anticipate the pressure before it's applied."

The sun dipped lower, casting long shadows of the four figures across the grass, a family bound by the roar of jets and the silence of a perfectly executed pass. The family was often seen at the airport: MuaBana, immaculate in her pilot uniform, dropping her sons off for a practice, or rushing back from a transatlantic flight to watch a major match. Her life was a testament to the fact that single motherhood was not a limitation, but a source of profound strength.

*****

The ultimate testament to her life came just as MuaBana, now in her fifties, was preparing for a routine flight to Frankfurt.

The news flashed across a large screen in the lounge: all three of her sons had not only been recruited by elite European soccer clubs but had just received their first joint call-up to the U.S. Men's National Soccer Team.

The boys' success was the final, indelible signature on her life's work. They were her trophy, her legacy, and the final proof that her choice had been the right one.

Captain MuaBana Bibishbo was still the pillar of her extended family, frequently traveling to the Congo to oversee her parents' care. Her father, now frail and softened by age, watched his grandsons play via satellite link, his pride undeniable.

He gave her a final, silent sign of acceptance by returning her childhood soccer medals and admitting, "You never needed a master plan, MuaBana. You were your own Captain from the start."

MuaBana had shown the world that a woman does not need a traditional structure to be great, nor a husband to be blessed. She had built her castle with her own two hands, raised her champions, and kept her gaze fixed on the horizon. Her life was full, rich, and utterly on her own terms.

She checked her watch, adjusted her captain's cap, and boarded her flight. Captain MuaBana Bibishbo had a sky to command, and a world where her sons would soar.